The Swing Era
1937-1938

EDITOR: Jay Gold

Staff for THE SWING ERA 1937-1938 EDITOR: Philip W. Payne ADMINISTRATIVE EDITOR: Jeanne LeMonnier
ASSISTANT EDITORS: David Johnson, Joan S. Reiter GRAPHICS: Leonard S. Levine RESEARCHERS: Lea Guyer,
Florence McNeil, Joan Nierenberg, Karl F. Reuling, Barbara Richey, Eleanor Schwartz, Jean Sulzberger, Michèle Wood
COPYREADER: Rachel Tuckerman CONSULTANTS: Dan Sibley (graphics), George T. Simon (editorial)

MANAGING DIRECTOR: Francis M. Scott III
GENERAL MANAGER: Peter L. Hoyt PROMOTION MANAGER: William C. Kiefer
INTERNATIONAL OPERATIONS MANAGER: Charles C. Colt, Jr.
EUROPEAN MANAGER: Robert H. Smith ASIA MANAGER: Beto Yamanouchi

THE SWING ERA is produced in the United States by TIME-LIFE RECORDS in cooperation with CAPITOL RECORDS,
INC. David D. Cavanaugh, Executive Producer, Bill Miller, Associate Producer. Editions outside the United States and
Canada are produced in cooperation with Electric & Musical Industries, Limited, London, England, or its affiliated companies.

ON THE COVER: A "break" in the Lindy Hop is shown in this high-speed action picture taken in 1943 by LIFE photographer
Gjon Mili. Dancers Kaye Popp and Stanley Catron demonstrate the dance, named originally for Lindbergh's 1927 flight to Paris.

The Swing Era

Vintage Years of Humor

The Men Who Made the Music:
- Artie Shaw
- Glen Gray
- Raymond Scott

The Music in This Volume

Discography

1937-1938

TIME-LIFE RECORDS
NEW YORK

Vintage Years of Humor:
An Anthology

DRAWING BY GEO. PRICE; COPR. © 1947
THE NEW YORKER MAGAZINE, INC.

DRAWING BY ALAIN; COPR. © 1937, 1965
THE NEW YORKER MAGAZINE, INC.

Modern Conveniences

"Our automatic record changer says
if it isn't Bach—to hell with it!"

"Help!"

THE SATURDAY EVENING POST

"Here it is! It says, 'To stop,
push forward left-hand lever on crossbar.'"

"Mind if I get in with you?
I think I've got a short circuit."

How is it that we discover in retrospect that so many funny things happened to us on our way through the Swing Era years of war and depression? Perhaps humor is an antidote—the belly laugh to cure the bellyache. Certainly the Swing Era coincided with the flowering of so many comic geniuses that every anthology of the period, including the one that makes up the first section of this volume, omits as many gems as it includes. There were so many gems. Several national magazines were devoted solely to humor, and many others leavened every issue with funny words and pictures.

As the following pages show, much of the humor of these vintage years retains its pith and tang because we were so willing then to laugh at ourselves. Jokes about the funny foreigner overseas or the stupid stranger in our midst tend to sour with age. The fun we poke at ourselves matures better.

In the Swing Era we happily kidded our whole society and all its products, including ourselves. Will Cuppy and Robert Benchley took solemn scientists down a peg. Gardner Rea, Ned Hilton and Rube Goldberg reduced the vast complexities of industry to charming muddles. James Thurber and E. B. White led us gently into the mazes of the human mind and left us there, lost and laughing. Peter Arno, with sophisticated savagery, and Charles Addams, with mad logic, chilled our gizzards, all in good fun.

We laughed in sympathy with H. T. Webster's Timid Soul and Helen Hokinson's pottering matrons; with J. R. Williams' dusty cowhands, grimy machinists and harried mothers, and with Baker's Sad Sack and Sgt. Bill Mauldin's Willie and Joe. They were all part of the family. Franklin P. Adams struggling in verse with a railroad timetable or Ogden Nash revealing in rueful rhyme a father's fantasies about his daughter's future suitors were joshing us along with themselves.

Like swing, the vintage humor of the Swing Era was not only great in its own time but has endured the test of time since then.

—THE EDITORS OF TIME-LIFE RECORDS

Signal Service

by Franklin P. Adams

Time-table! Terrible and hard
    To figure! At some station lonely
We see this sign upon the card:
    *

We read thee wrong; the untrained eye
    Does not see always with precision.
The train we thought to travel by
    †

Again, undaunted, we look at
    The hieroglyphs, and as a rule a
Small double dagger shows us that
    ‡

And when we take a certain line
    On Tues., Wednes., Thurs., Fri., Sat., or Monday,
We're certain to detect the sign:
    §

Heck Junction—Here she comes! Fft! Whiz!
    A scurry—and the train has flitted!
Again we look. We find it—viz.
    ||

Through hieroglyphic seas we wade—
    Print is so cold and so unfeeling.
The train we await at Neverglade
    ¶

Now hungrily the sheet we scan
    Grimy with travel, thirsty, weary,
And then—nothing is sadder than
    ☞

Yet, cursèd as is every sign,
    The cussedest that we can quote is
This treacherous and deadly line:
    ⁂

---

  * Train 20: stops on signal only.
  † Runs only on North-west division.
  ‡ Train does not stop at Ashtabula.
  § $10 extra fare ex. Sunday.
  || Train does not stop where time omitted.
  ¶ Connects with C. & A. at Wheeling.
  ☞ No diner on till after Erie.
  ⁂ Subject to change without our notice.

Why We Laugh—or Do We?
(Let's Get This Thing Settled, Mr. Eastman)

by Robert Benchley

In order to laugh at something, it is necessary (1) to know *what* you are laughing at, (2) to know *why* you are laughing, (3) to ask some people why *they* think you are laughing, (4) to jot down a few notes, (5) to laugh. Even then, the thing may not be cleared up for days.

All laughter is merely a compensatory reflex to take the place of sneezing. What we really want to do is sneeze, but as that is not always possible, we laugh instead. Sometimes we underestimate our powers and laugh and sneeze at the same time. This raises hell all around.

The old phrase "That is nothing to sneeze at" proves my point. What is obviously meant is "That is nothing to *laugh* at." The wonder is that nobody ever thought of this explanation of laughter before, with the evidence staring him in the face like that.*

We sneeze because we are thwarted, discouraged, or devil-may-care. Failing a sneeze, we laugh, *faute de mieux.* Analyze any funny story or comic situation at which we "laugh" and it will be seen that this theory is correct. Incidentally, by the time you have the "humor" analyzed, it will be found that the necessity for laughing has been relieved.

Let us take the well-known joke about the man who put the horse in the bathroom.** Here we have a perfect example of the thought-sneeze process, or, if you will, the sneeze-thought process. The man, obviously

---

  *Schwanzleben, in his work "Humor After Death," hits on this point indirectly when he says, "All laughter is a muscular rigidity spasmodically relieved by involuntary twitching. It can be induced by the application of electricity as well as by a so-called 'joke.' "

  **A man who lived in a boarding house brought a horse home with him one night, led it upstairs, and shut it in the bathroom. The landlady, aroused by the commotion, protested, pointed to the broken balustrade, the torn stair carpet, and the obvious maladjustment of the whole thing, and asked the man, confidentially, just why he had seen fit to shut a horse in the common bathroom. To which the man replied, "In the morning, the boarders, one by one, will go into the bathroom, and will come rushing out, exclaiming, 'There's a *horse* in the bathroom!' I want to be able to say, 'Yes, I know.' "

an introvert, was motivated by a will-to-dominate-the-bathroom, combined with a desire to be superior to the other boarders. The humor of the situation may *seem* to us to lie in the tag line "I want to be able to say, 'Yes, I know,'" but we laugh at the joke *subconsciously* long before this line comes in. In fact, what we are really laughing (or sneezing) at is the idea of someone's telling us a joke that we have heard before.

Let us suppose that the story was reversed, and that a *horse* had put a *man* into the bathroom. Then our laughter would have been induced by the idea of a landlady's asking a horse a question and the horse's answering—an entirely different form of joke.

The man would then have been left in the bathroom with nothing to do with the story. Likewise, if the man had put the *landlady* into the bathroom, the *horse* would obviously have been *hors de combat* (still another form of joke, playing on the similarity in sound between the word "horse" and the French word *"hors,"* meaning *"out* of." Give up?).

Any joke, besides making us want to sneeze, must have five cardinal points, and we must check up on these first before giving in:

(1) The joke must be in a language we can understand.

(2) It must be spoken loudly enough for us to hear it, or printed clearly enough for us to read it.

(3) It must be about *something*. You can't just say, "Here's a good joke" and let it go at that. (You *can*, but don't wait for the laugh.)

(4) It must deal with either frustration or accomplishment, inferiority or superiority, sense or nonsense, pleasantness or unpleasantness, or, at any rate, with some emotion that can be analyzed, otherwise how do we know when to laugh?

(5) It must begin with the letter "W."*

Now, let us see just how our joke about the horse in the bathroom fulfills these specifications. Using the *Gestalt*, or Rotary-Frictional, method of taking the skin off a joke, we can best illustrate by making a diagram of it. We have seen that every joke must be in a language that we can understand and spoken (or written) so clearly that we can hear it (or see it). Otherwise we have this:

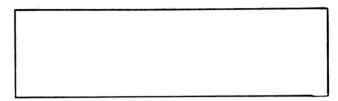

Fig. 1.
Joke which we cannot hear, see, or understand the words of.

You will see in Figure 2 that we go upstairs with the man and the horse as far as the bathroom. Here we become conscious that it is not a *true* story, something we may have suspected all along but didn't want to say anything about. This sudden revelation of *absurdity* (from the Latin *ab* and *surdus*, meaning "out of deafness") is represented in the diagram by an old-fashioned whirl.

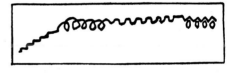

Fig. 2.
The horse-in-the-bathroom story under ideal conditions.

Following the shock of realization that the story is not real, we progress in the diagram to the point where the landlady protests. Here we come to an actual *fact*, or factual *act*. Any landlady in her right mind *would* protest against a horse's being shut in her bathroom. So we have, in the diagram, a return to normal ratiocination or Crowther's Disease, represented by the wavy line. (Whoo-hoo!)

From then on, it is anybody's joke. The whole thing becomes just ludicrous. This we can show in the diagram by the egg-and-dart design, making it clear that something has definitely gone askew. Personally, I think that what the man *meant* to say was "That's no horse—that's my wife," but that he was inhibited. (Some of these jokes even *I* can't seem to get through my head.)*

---

*Gunfy, in his "Laughter Considered as a Joint Disease," holds that the letter "W" is not essential to the beginning of a joke, so long as it comes in somewhere before the joke is over. However, tests made on five hundred subjects in the Harvard School of Applied Laughter, using the Mergenthaler Laugh Detector, have shown that, unless a joke begins with the letter "W," the laughter is forced, almost unpleasant at times.

---

*A. E. Bassinette, in his pamphlet "What Is Humor—a Joke?," claims to have discovered a small tropical fly which causes laughter. This fly, according to this authority, was carried from Central America back to Spain by Columbus's men, and spread from there to the rest of Europe, returning to America, on a visit, in 1667, on a man named George Altschuh.

The Night the Bed Fell

by James Thurber

I suppose that the high-water mark of my youth in Columbus, Ohio, was the night the bed fell on my father. It makes a better recitation (unless, as some friends of mine have said, one has heard it five or six times) than it does a piece of writing, for it is almost necessary to throw furniture around, shake doors, and bark like a dog, to lend the proper atmosphere and verisimilitude to what is admittedly a somewhat incredible tale. Still, it did take place.

It happened, then, that my father had decided to sleep in the attic one night, to be away where he could think. My mother opposed the notion strongly because, she said, the old wooden bed up there was unsafe; it was wobbly and the heavy headboard would crash down on father's head in case the bed fell, and kill him. There was no dissuading him, however, and at a quarter past ten he closed the attic door behind him and went up the narrow twisting stairs. We later heard ominous creakings as he crawled into bed. Grandfather, who usually slept in the attic bed when he was with us, had disappeared some days before. (On these occasions he was usually gone six or eight days and returned growling and out of temper, with the news that the federal Union was run by a passel of blockheads and that the Army of the Potomac didn't have any more chance than a fiddler's bitch.)

We had visiting us at this time a nervous first cousin of mine named Briggs Beall, who believed that he was likely to cease breathing when he was asleep. It was his feeling that if he were not awakened every hour during the night, he might die of suffocation. He had been accustomed to setting an alarm clock to ring at intervals until morning, but I persuaded him to abandon this. He slept in my room and I told him that I was such a light sleeper that if anybody quit breathing in the same room with me, I would wake instantly. He tested me the first night—which I had suspected he would—by holding his breath after my regular breathing had convinced him I was asleep. I was not asleep, however, and called to him. This seemed to allay his fears a little, but he took the precaution of putting a glass of spirits of camphor on a little table at the head of his bed. In case I didn't arouse him until he was almost gone, he said, he would sniff the camphor, a powerful reviver. Briggs was not the only member of his family who had his crotchets. Old Aunt Melissa Beall (who could whistle like a man, with two fingers in her mouth) suffered under the premonition that she was destined to die on South High Street, because she had been born on South High Street and married on South High Street. Then there was Aunt Sarah Shoaf, who never went to bed at night without the fear that a burglar was going to get in and blow chloroform under her door through a tube. To avert this calamity—for she was in greater dread of anesthetics than of losing her household goods—she always piled her money, silverware, and other valuables in a neat stack just outside her bedroom, with a note reading: "This is all I have. Please take it and do not use your chloroform, as this is all I have." Aunt Gracie Shoaf also had a burglar phobia, but she met it with more fortitude. She was confident that burglars had been getting into her house every night for forty years. The fact that she never missed anything was to her no proof to the contrary. She always claimed that she scared them off before they could take anything, by throwing shoes down the hallway. When she went to bed she piled, where she could get at them handily, all the shoes there were about her house. Five minutes after she had turned off the light, she would sit up in bed and say "Hark!" Her husband, who had learned to ignore the whole situation as long ago as 1903, would either be sound asleep or pretend to be sound asleep. In either case he would not respond to her tugging and pulling, so that presently she would arise, tiptoe to the door, open it slightly and heave a shoe down the hall in one direction, and its mate down the hall in the other direction. Some nights she threw them all, some nights only a couple of pair.

But I am straying from the remarkable incidents that took place during the night that the bed fell on father.

Some Nights She Threw Them All

By midnight we were all in bed. The layout of the rooms and the disposition of their occupants is important to an understanding of what later occurred. In the front room upstairs (just under father's attic bedroom) were my mother and my brother Herman, who sometimes sang in his sleep, usually "Marching Through Georgia" or "Onward, Christian Soldiers." Briggs Beall and myself were in a room adjoining this one. My brother Roy was in a room across the hall from ours. Our bull terrier, Rex, slept in the hall.

My bed was an army cot, one of those affairs which are made wide enough to sleep on comfortably only by putting up, flat with the middle section, the two sides which ordinarily hang down like the sideboards of a drop-leaf table. When these sides are up, it is perilous to roll too far toward the edge, for then the cot is likely to tip completely over, bringing the whole bed down on top of one, with a tremendous banging crash. This, in fact, is precisely what happened, about two o'clock in the morning. (It was my mother who, in recalling the scene later, first referred to it as "the night the bed fell on your father.")

Always a deep sleeper, slow to arouse (I had lied to Briggs), I was at first unconscious of what had happened when the iron cot rolled me onto the floor and toppled over on me. It left me still warmly bundled up and unhurt, for the bed rested above me like a canopy. Hence I did not wake up, only reached the edge of consciousness and went back. The racket, however, instantly awakened my mother, in the next room, who came to the immediate conclusion that her worst dread was realized: the big wooden bed upstairs had fallen on father. She therefore screamed, "Let's go to your poor father!" It was this shout, rather than the noise of my cot falling, that awakened Herman, in the same room with her. He thought that mother had become, for no apparent reason, hysterical. "You're all right, Mamma!" he shouted, trying to calm her. They exchanged shout for shout for perhaps ten seconds: "Let's go to your poor father!" and "You're all right!" That woke up Briggs. By this time I was conscious of what was going on, in a vague way, but did not yet realize that I was under my bed instead of on it. Briggs, awakening in the midst of loud shouts of fear and apprehension, came to the quick conclusion that he was suffocating and that we were all trying to "bring him out." With a low moan, he grasped the glass of camphor at the head of his bed and instead of sniffing it poured it over himself. The room reeked of camphor. "Ugf, ahfg," choked Briggs, like a drowning man, for he had almost succeeded in stopping his breath under the deluge of pungent spirits. He leaped out of bed and groped toward the open window, but he came up against one that was closed. With his hand, he beat out the glass, and I could hear it crash and tinkle on the alleyway below. It was at this juncture that I, in

trying to get up, had the uncanny sensation of feeling my bed above me! Foggy with sleep, I now suspected, in my turn, that the whole uproar was being made in a frantic endeavor to extricate me from what must be an unheard-of and perilous situation. "Get me out of this!" I bawled. "Get me out!" I think I had the nightmarish belief that I was entombed in a mine. "Gugh," gasped Briggs, floundering in his camphor.

By this time my mother, still shouting, pursued by Herman, still shouting, was trying to open the door to

He Came to the Conclusion That He Was Suffocating

the attic, in order to go up and get my father's body out of the wreckage. The door was stuck, however, and wouldn't yield. Her frantic pulls on it only added to the general banging and confusion. Roy and the dog were now up, the one shouting questions, the other barking.

Father, farthest away and soundest sleeper of all, had by this time been awakened by the battering on the attic door. He decided that the house was on fire. "I'm coming, I'm coming!" he wailed in a slow, sleepy voice—it took him many minutes to regain full consciousness. My mother, still believing he was caught under the bed, detected in his "I'm coming!" the mournful, resigned note of one who is preparing to meet his Maker. "He's dying!" she shouted.

"I'm all right!" Briggs yelled to reassure her. "I'm all right!" He still believed that it was his own closeness to death that was worrying mother. I found at last the light switch in my room, unlocked the door, and Briggs and I joined the others at the attic door. The dog, who never did like Briggs, jumped for him—assuming that he was the culprit in whatever was going on—and Roy had to throw Rex and hold him. We could hear father crawling out of bed upstairs. Roy pulled the attic door open, with a mighty jerk, and father came down the stairs, sleepy and irritable but safe and sound. My mother began to weep when she saw him. Rex began to howl. "What in the name of God is going on here?" asked father.

The situation was finally put together like a gigantic jig-saw puzzle. Father caught a cold from prowling around in his bare feet but there were no other bad results. "I'm glad," said mother, who always looked on the bright side of things, "that your grandfather wasn't here."

Answers to Hard Questions

by E. B. White

Dear Mrs. Post——When we have two women guests and they sit at the right and left of my husband and our two half-grown children at the right and left of me, how should the maid serving proceed around the table? When the guest of honor at the right of my husband is served first, if the maid has to walk around him to serve the lady on his left next, the extra time consumed makes service even slower. And yet, if she starts with the lady at the right of my husband and goes around the table to the right, serving my husband last, she also serves the second lady to everything after the choicest pieces are gone. What would you suggest?——*From Emily Post's column in the Boston Globe.*

The key to this situation is the two half-grown children. No matter what sort of erratic course a maid may pursue around a dinner table, the eyes of a half-grown child will follow her, as though by magnetic influence. This grim gaze contributes to the general feeling of the passage of time. Conversation drags, finally dies. Only the steady tramp-tramp-tramp of the maid and the harsh click of serving spoon against dish relieve the silence. Sometimes an unusually quick half-grown child will reach out a hand as the dish is going by and take something off it. This lessens the actual time consumed in serving the meal, but on the whole there is no satisfactory way of routing a waitress at such a gathering. Guests and hostess alike must simply resign themselves to the fact that the household is understaffed and the party ill-conceived. All dinners end at last, and this one will, too.

Dear Sisters—Can any of you tell me how to keep my dog from making his bed on the dining room table. As soon as we go out or go to bed he gets on it.—— *Letter in the Boston Globe.*

With a dog like that you should never go out, and you should never go to bed. Stay in, and stay up.

L.D. writes: Is there any likelihood that the temporary physical condition a man is in would have an effect on his offspring? In other words, should a man hesitate about becoming a father during the time he is suffering from hay fever?——*Health column in the Chicago Tribune.*

This is a question many a man has had to face, alone with his God. Sensitivity to pollen, the male element of flowers, is at once an exalted and a pitiable condition and inevitably suggests to a prospective progenitor the disquieting potentialities inherent in all propagation. Like father like son is the familiar saying: big sneeze, little sneeze. There is little doubt that allergy to hay, so deep-seated, so shattering, is inheritable; and it is just as certain that a sensitive man, during the season of his great distress, is as eager for life and love as in the periods when his mucosae are relaxed. We cannot conscientiously advise any man to abstain from fatherhood on a seasonal, or foliage, basis. The time not to become a father is eighteen years before a world war.

Miss F.: How does one announce a secret marriage, when the bride does not live at home?——*Vogue.*

There is only one correct way to announce a secret marriage, no matter where the bride lives. Use invisible ink.

"Herman! What's come over you?"

Q. When a man does not believe in tipping and is eating in a place where tipping is customary, what should he do?——*Letter to the Charleroi (Pa.) Mail.*

Tip.

Phobias

by Robert Benchley

The discovery of phobias by the psychiatrists has done much to clear the atmosphere. Whereas in the old days a person would say: "Let's get the heck out of here!" today he says: "Let's get the heck out of here! I've got claustrophobia!"

Most everybody knows the name of the phobia that he has personally, and it is a great comfort to him. If he is afraid of high places, he just says: "Oh, it's just my old acrophobia," and jumps.

If he is afraid of being alone he knows that he has monophobia and has the satisfaction of knowing that he is a pathological case. If he keeps worrying, in the middle of a meal, about the possibility of being buried alive, he can flatter himself that he has taphephobia, and that it is no worse than a bad cold.

❋ ❋ ❋ ❋ ❋

But there are some honeys among the phobias that don't get much publicity. There is, for example, phobophobia, which is the fear of having a phobia, even though you may not have one at the moment. This takes the form of the patient sitting in terror and saying to himself: "Supposing I should be afraid of food, I would starve to death!" Not a very pretty picture, you will admit.

Then there is kemophobia, or the fear of sitting too close to the edge of a chair and falling off. People with kemophobia are constantly hitching themselves back in their chairs until they tip themselves over backward. This gives the same general effect as falling off the chair frontward, so they find themselves in a *cul-de-sac.*

Then there is goctophobia, or the fear of raising the hand too far and striking oneself in the face, with the possibility of putting an eye out. These patients keep their hands in their pockets all the time and have to be fed by paid attendants. A nasty complication arises when they also have nictophobia, or fear of paid attendants.

The Sexes

"I wonder if you could give me an estimate, Myrtle, about how much it would cost to support you per year?"

"Now, not so fast. . . . Look out for this corner! . . . Turn left at the tomatoes. . . . Slower. . . . Look out for that bump. Oh, Oh!"

Some of the other little known phobias are octophobia, or fear of the figure 8; genophobia, or the fear of being burned on door-handles; kneebophobia, or the fear that one knee is going to bend backwards instead of forwards some day, and optophobia, or the dread of opening the eyes for fear of what they will see.

Tell us your phobias and we will tell you what you are afraid of.

Memoirs of the Jukes Family or Where We Come In

by Will Cuppy

THE JAVA MAN

The Java Man lived in Java 500,000 or 1,000,000 or 2,000,000 years ago[1] and was lower than we are. He was Lower Pleistocene and Lower Quarternary and knock-kneed. He was called *Pithecanthropus* ("Ape-Man") *erectus* because he walked with a slight stoop. The Java Man consisted of a calvarium, three teeth and a femur belonging to himself or two other Ape-Men. Professor Dubois made him a face which proves that he was dolichocephalic or long-headed instead of brachycephalic or square-headed and that he was 5 feet 6½ inches high and that Barnum was right. The Java Man was more Manlike than Apelike and more Apelike than Manlike. He had immense supraorbital ridges of solid bone and was conscious in spots. Does that remind you of any one?[2] His Broca's area was low. He could say

---

[1] Or 250,000 or 750,000.

[2] Sir Arthur Keith says that *Pithecanthropus erectus* was human in everything but the brain. Well, what did he expect?

---

that the evenings were drawing in and times were hard and his feet hurt. The spiritual life of the Java Man was low because he was only a beginner. He was just a child at heart and was perfectly satisfied with his polygamy, polygyny, polyandry, endogamy, exogamy, totemism and nymphomania. How he ever became extinct is beyond me. The Java Man has been called the Missing Link by those who should know.

THE PEKING MAN

The Peking Man shows that people were living in Asia long long ago as most of us knew already. He was discovered near Peking or Peiping and was named *Sinanthropus pekinensis* to keep certain persons from calling him Peiping Tom. *Sin* means China although the Chinese are no worse than other foreigners. The glabella was prominent so he was probably a young male.[1] The brain shows that the calvarium or braincase was good. The skull was in perfect condition because the Peking Man took better care of his skull than some of us. He had begun to think or whatever the Chinese do. The prefrontal region resembles that found in some parts of the Middle West. The right horizontal ramus shows a tendency to do everything backwards. The Peking Man is lovable because he left no culture. He knew nothing about the Ming Dynasty and the Ch'ing Dynasty and the Sung Dynasty and he wrote no short poems stating that he got drunk and went out in a canoe and fell in. He had no imports and exports but he had fauna and flora.[2] The Peking

---

[1] Or a young female.

[2] He had the Catalpa, the Soy Bean, the Mongolian Mammoth, the Chinese Ostrich, the Yak and the Carp. He may have had Bats.

Man was fond of overpopulation. We do not know whether he was religious or promiscuous or both. He did not have love as we understand it because he had no gin.

THE PILTDOWN MAN

The Piltdown Man was called the Dawn Man or Barmy Ned because he was found in Great Britain. He was a great help because he left crude flint implements. These were small rough pebbles chipped by the Piltdown Man just as all the small rough pebbles of today were chipped by us. Crude flint implements were used for making still cruder flint implements.[1] The Piltdown Man had little to do. His skull was twice as thick as an ordinary Englishman. It is in small pieces which can be fitted together in various ways after choosing sides. This is called Badminton. He could collect stamps. The Piltdown Man had aspidistras, delphiniums and sinus trouble. Already he was aiming at the stars and missing them. The manubrium indicates self-control but very little to control. The Piltdown Man had no chin and was rather toothy. It seems incredible that he had a private life but those are just the ones who do. The young took after their parents. Anthropologists say that the Piltdown Man was stupider than any person of today. Anthropologists are people who are in museums. They lead sheltered lives. The Early Irish left few skulls. The Early Scotch left no skulls.

[1] Some say the Piltdown Man also used them to scrape furs if he had furs, for clothing if he had clothing. It is not improbable that the better sort of Piltdown Men employed some form of covering, if only a minimum.

THE MODERN MAN

The Modern Man or Nervous Wreck is the highest of all mammals because anyone can see that he is. There are about 2,000,000,000 Modern Men or too many. The Modern Man's highly developed brain has made him what he is and you know what he is.[1] The development of his brain is caused by his upright or bipedal position, as in the Penguin, the Dinosaur and other extinct reptiles. Modern Man has been called the Talking Animal because he talks more than any three other animals chosen at random. He has also been called the Reasoning Animal but there may be a catch in this. The fissure of Sylvius and the fissure of Rolando enable him to argue in circles. His main pursuits in the order named are murder, robbery, kidnapping, body-snatching, barratry, nepotism, arson and mayhem. This is known as the Good, the True and the Beautiful. Modern Men are viviparous. They mature slowly but make up for it later, generally from July first to June thirtieth inclusive. The females carry nickels and pins in their mouths. They are fond of glittering objects, bits of ribbon and olives.[2] All Modern Men are descended from a Wormlike creature but it shows more on some people. Modern Man will never become extinct if the Democrats can help it.[3]

[1] It is because of his brain that he has risen above the animals. Guess which animals he has risen above.

[2] Each male has from 2 to 790 females with whom he discusses current events. Of these he marries from 3 to 17.

[3] To be perfectly fair, Modern Man was invented on October 25, 4004 B.C., at 9 o'clock in the morning, according to the statement of Dr. John Lightfoot (1602–1675) of Stoke-upon-Trent, Vicechancellor of the University of Cambridge. Dr. Lightfoot's *Whole Works* comes in thirteen volumes.

Father and Margaret

by Clarence Day

One late afternoon when Father came up from downtown, he found his home much upset. Our cook had walked out and left us. I was a child of four, George was two, and there was a new baby besides. Mother was ill. She hadn't been able to leave us to go to an agency. And as she was no hand at cooking herself, the outlook for dinner was poor.

This state of affairs was unprecedented in all Father's experience. In his father's home, they never changed their servants suddenly; they seldom changed them at all; and as his mother was a past mistress of cooking, he had always been doubly protected. Since his marriage, he had had to live a much bumpier life. But this was the worst yet.

He asked Mother, who was lying in bed, what she was going to do about it. There were no telephones then, and she couldn't do anything at all, at the moment; but she said she would try to go to an agency in the morning and see what she could find. "In the morning? Good God!" Father said. "Where is the place, anyhow?" And he clapped on his hat and strode out again, over toward Sixth Avenue.

As I heard the story years afterward, it was late when he got there, and he bounded up the front stoop two or three steps at a time, and went quickly into the little office, where the gaslights were burning. He had never been in such a place before, and to his surprise it was empty, except for a severe-looking woman who sat at a desk at one side. "Where do you keep 'em?" he urgently demanded, his mind on the question of dinner.

She looked at him, got out her pen, and opened a large book deliberately. "I will take your name and address," she informed him, "and then, if you please, you may give me the details as to what kind of person you require and when you would wish her to call."

But Father had no time, he told her, for any damned fol-de-rol. "Where do you keep 'em?" he said again. She was standing in the way of his dinner. I can imagine how his face must have reddened and how his eyes must have blazed at her. "I am asking you where you keep them!" he roared.

"Why, the girls are in there," the lady explained, to calm him, "but clients are not allowed in that room. If you will tell me the kind of position you wish me to fill for you, I will have one come out."

Before she'd half finished, Father had thrown open the door and gone in. There sat a crowd of the girls, young and old, sickly and brawny, of all shapes and sizes; some ugly, some pretty and trim and stylish, some awkward; nurses, ladies' maids, waitresses, washerwomen, and cooks.

Youth

"If I write a great novel and they make a movie of it, they might put Mr. Gable in it, and then maybe I'll get to meet him!"

The manager was by now at Father's elbow, trying to make him get out, and insisting that he tell her the position he wished her to fill. But Father was swiftly glancing around at the crowd, and he paid no attention. He noticed a little woman in the corner, with honest gray eyes, who sat there, shrewd-looking and quiet. He pointed his cane over at her and said, "I'll take that one."

The manager was flustered, but still she kept trying to enforce her authority. She protested she didn't yet know the position. . . .

"Cook," Father said, "cook."

"But Margaret doesn't wish to be a cook, she wants—"

"You can cook, can't you?" Father demanded.

Margaret's plain little face was still pink with excitement and pleasure at being chosen above all that roomful by such a masterful gentleman. Father had probably smiled at her, too, for they liked each other at once. Well, she said, she had cooked for one family.

"Of course she can cook," Father said.

He said afterward, when describing the incident, "I knew at once she could cook."

The manager didn't like this at all. The discipline of the office was spoiled. "If you are going to take her anyhow," she said acidly, "what day would you wish her to come, and will you please give me your name?"

"Oh, this is nothing. I was drinking before repeal."

"Yes, yes," Father said, without giving it. "Come on, Margaret." And he planked down the fee and walked out.

Margaret followed him through the door and trotted over to our home at his heels. He sent her down to the kitchen immediately, while he went upstairs to dress.

"I don't know why you make such a fuss about engaging new servants. It's simple enough," he said comfortably to Mother that evening, after Margaret's first dinner.

It was the first of a long series, for she stayed with us twenty-six years.

Old Margaret was just the kind of cook that we wanted. Lots of cooks can do rich dishes well. Margaret couldn't. But she cooked simple, everyday dishes in a way that made our mouths water. Her apple pies were the most satisfying pies I've ever tasted. Her warmed-up potatoes were so delicious I could have made my whole dinner of them.

"I hope, dear, you won't come back from Vassar with a lot of ideas."

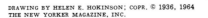

"You ought to see Albert's new car—the seat folds back and makes a bed!"

Yet even Margaret sometimes miscalculated. A large, royal-looking steak would be set before Father, which, upon being cut into, would turn out to be too underdone. Father's face would darken with disappointment. If the earth had begun to wobble and reel in its orbit he could scarcely have been more disapproving. He would raise his foot, under the table, and stamp slowly and heavily three times on the rug. Thud; thud; thud.

At this solemn signal, we would hear Margaret leave

Father and Margaret were united by the intense interest they both took in cooking. Each understood the other instinctively. They had a complete fellow-feeling. Mother's great interest was in babies—she had never been taught how to cook. All she wanted was to keep Father pleased somehow; and if it was too difficult she didn't always care about even that.

At table it was Father who carved the fowl, or sliced the roast lamb or beef. I liked to watch him whet the

Industry

CAPTAINS OF INDUSTRY

Mr. Rand and Mr. McNally find themselves at an uncharted crossroad.

Mr. Pullman discovers one of his towels in his host's bathroom

the kitchen below us and come clumping step by step up the stairs to the dining-room door.

"Margaret, look at that steak."

Margaret would step nearer and peer with a shocked look at the platter. "The Lord bless us and save us," she would say to herself in a low voice. She would then seize the platter and make off with it, to better it the best way she could, and Father would gloomily wait and eat a few vegetables and pour out a fresh glass of claret.

knife and go at it. He had such a fine, easy hand. To a hungry boy, he seemed overdeliberate and exact in his strokes, yet in a moment or two he had done. And usually the cooking had been as superb as the carving. Sometimes it was so perfect that Father's face would crinkle with pleasure, and with a wink at us he'd summon Margaret with his usual three measured thumps. She would appear, clutching her skirts with both hands, and looking worried. "What's wanting?" she'd ask.

"Margaret," Father would tell her affectionately, "that fricasseed chicken is *good*."

Margaret would turn her wrinkled face aside, and look down, and push the flat of her hand out toward Father. It was the same gesture she used when she said "Get along with you" to flatterers. She couldn't say that to Father, but she would beam at him, and turn and go out, and stump back down the dark little stairs without ever a word.

CAPTAINS OF INDUSTRY
Mr. Wurlitzer's mighty console fails to rise.

Long after Margaret died, Father was speaking one night of how good her things always had tasted.

"I wish she could hear you," said Mother. She smiled tenderly at the thought of that gallant and dear little figure. "If anybody ever was sure of going to Heaven," she added, "I know it was Margaret."

This struck Father as a recommendation of the place. He took a sip of cognac and said casually, "I'll look her up when I get there. I'll have her take care of me."

Mother started to say something but checked herself. "What's the matter?" he asked.

"Well, Clare dear," said Mother, "Margaret must be in some special part of Heaven, she was so good. You'd be very fortunate, Clare, to get to the same part as Margaret."

"Hah!" Father said, suddenly scowling. "I'll make a devil of a row if I don't."

The Unicorn in the Garden

by James Thurber

Once upon a sunny morning a man who sat in a breakfast nook looked up from his scrambled eggs to see a white unicorn with a gold horn quietly cropping the roses in the garden. The man went up to the bedroom where his wife was still asleep and woke her. "There's a unicorn in the garden," he said. "Eating roses." She opened one unfriendly eye and looked at him. "The unicorn is a mythical beast," she said, and turned her back on him. The man walked slowly downstairs and out into the garden. The unicorn was still there; he was now browsing among the tulips. "Here, unicorn," said the man, and he pulled up a lily and gave it to him. The unicorn ate it gravely. With a high heart, because there was a unicorn in his garden, the man went upstairs and roused his wife again. "The unicorn," he said, "ate a lily." His wife sat up in bed and looked at him, coldly. "You are a booby," she said, "and I am going to have you put in the booby-hatch." The man, who had never liked the words "booby" and "booby-hatch," and who liked them even less on a shining morning when there was a unicorn in the garden, thought for a moment. "We'll see about that," he said. He walked over to the door. "He has a golden horn in the middle of his forehead," he told her. Then he went back to the garden to watch the unicorn; but the unicorn had gone away. The man sat down among the roses and went to sleep.

As soon as the husband had gone out of the house, the wife got up and dressed as fast as she could. She was very excited and there was a gloat in her eye. She telephoned the police and she telephoned a psychiatrist; she told them to hurry to her house and bring a straitjacket. When the police and the psychiatrist arrived they sat down in chairs and looked at her, with great interest. "My husband," she said, "saw a unicorn this morning." The police looked at the psychiatrist and the psychiatrist looked at the police. "He told me it ate a lily," she said. The psychiatrist looked at the police and the police looked at the psychiatrist. "He told me it had a golden horn in the middle of its forehead," she said. At a solemn signal from the psychiatrist, the police leaped from their chairs and seized the wife. They had a hard time subduing her, for she put up a terrific struggle, but they finally subdued her. Just as they got her into the strait-jacket, the husband came back into the house.

"Did you tell your wife you saw a unicorn?" asked the police. "Of course not," said the husband. "The unicorn is a mythical beast." "That's all I wanted to know," said the psychiatrist. "Take her away. I'm sorry, sir, but your wife is as crazy as a jay bird." So they took her away, cursing and screaming, and shut her up in an institution. The husband lived happily ever after.

Moral: Don't count your boobies until they are hatched.

"Let's put 'Quail on toast' on today's menu. We can cross it off"

The Art of Story-Telling

by Robert Benchley

SCENE: A group in the living room before a dinner. Perhaps half of the guests have arrived, including Joe and Mrs. Joe. The hearth rug is already liberally sprinkled with grated egg from the canapes.

Mrs. Joe—Joe, tell them about you and Ed at the Moulin Rouge!

Joe—Oh, it's too long to tell now.

Mrs. Joe—No, it isn't. Go ahead!

Hostess—Go ahead, Joe. What was it?

Joe—Why, it wasn't anything at all.

Mrs. Joe—Oh, it was *so* funny. Don't be temperamental, Joe. Go ahead, tell it.

The Rest—Go ahead, Joe. Don't be so shy.

Joe—Oh, all right! Ed and I were in Paris and one night he said: "Let's go to the Moulin Rouge and see a little life—"

Wise Guy—See a little *life* or *wife?* (*General laughter.*)

Joe (*passing it off*)—Well, whichever you want . . . Anyway, we got there and, on the way in, there is a little bar, so Ed said—

(*Two more guests arrive and are introduced all around. They explain how they happened to be late. Joe starts to duck out quietly.*)

Hostess—Come back here, Joe! (*To new guests*) Joe was just telling about the time that he and Ed Bemis went to the Moulin Rouge in Paris . . . Go ahead, Joe.

Joe—Oh, I guess we'd better skip it. It's too long.

New Guests—Oh, no. Please go ahead.

The Rest—Go ahead, Joe. Don't be actory.

Joe—Well, anyway, Ed and I stopped off at this bar in the foyer of the Moulin Rouge—

Maid (*entering*)—Telephone for you, Mrs. Linker.

Hostess—It's probably the Deamons saying they're just starting. I'll be right back. Go ahead, Joe. I've heard it, anyway (*leaves the room*).

Wise Guy—Who hasn't? (*General laughter.*)

Joe (*laughing nervously*)—Well, I guess it's happened to most everyone. Well, anyway—just as we stopped at the bar—

(*Two more guests arrive and shake hands all around. They tell of an experience that happened to them on the way to dinner.*)

Joe (*concentrating on the woman next to him*)—So we stopped at the bar—

(*The hostess returns, and, in the general confusion, Joe escapes.*)

Wise Guy (*on way in to dinner*)—What is wrong with Joe? He always tries to monopolize the conversation.

Columbus

by Ogden Nash

Once upon a time there was an Italian,
And some people thought he was a rapscallion,
But he wasn't offended,
Because other people thought he was splendid,
And he said the world was round,
And everybody made an uncomplimentary sound,
But his only reply was Pooh,
He replied, Isn't this fourteen ninety-two?
It's time for me to discover America if I know my chronology.
And if I discover America you owe me an apology,
So he went and tried to borrow some money from Ferdinand

"What, dear? I can't hear a word with this patent crackling cereal."

© GREGORY D'ALESSIO

Our Daily Bread

But Ferdinand said America was a bird in the bush
    and he'd rather have a berdinand,
But Columbus' brain was fertile, it wasn't arid,
And he remembered that Ferdinand was married,
And he thought, there is no wife like a misunderstood
    one,
Because her husband thinks something is a terrible
    idea she is bound to think it a good one,
So he perfumed his handkerchief with bay rum and
    citronella,
And he went to see Isabella,
And he looked wonderful but he had never felt sillier,
And she said, I can't place the face but the aroma
    is familiar,
And Columbus didn't say a word,
All he said was, I am Columbus, the fifteenth-century
    Admiral Byrd,
And just as he thought, her disposition was very mal-
    leable,
And she said, Here are my jewels, and she wasn't pe-
    nurious like Cornelia the mother of the Gracchi,
    she wasn't referring to her children, no, she
    was referring to her jewels, which were very
    very valuable,
So Columbus said, somebody show me the sunset and
    somebody did and he set sail for it,
And he discovered America and they put him in jail
    for it,
And the fetters gave him welts,
And they named America after somebody else,
So the sad fate of Columbus ought to be pointed out
    to every child and every voter,
Because it has a very important moral, which is, Don't
    be a discoverer, be a promoter.

"It was your father's wish that there be no cranberry sauce."

"Good Lord! This is the one I shot—you're cooking the decoy!!"

Training for the Allen—Benny Fight

From a radio broadcast featuring Fred Allen, Portland Hoffa and Harry von Zell

by Fred Allen

PORTLAND   Are you going to train to fight Jack Benny?

ALLEN   Yes, Portland, I'll have to go on a pastry diet. I'll do some soft living to get in the same condition; I don't want to take an unfair advantage. Benny's as soft as a herd of goo.

HARRY   Jack said you had to starch your legs so they wouldn't wobble, Fred.

ALLEN   I don't have to wear a ramrod in the back of my vest to keep my spine from drooping. If Benny ever gets into the ring with me he'd better bring a taxidermist for his second. If I hit him once he'll be the life of the observation ward.

HARRY   What about Benny's muscles?

ALLEN   His arm looks like a buggy whip with fingers. I've got veins in my nose bigger than Benny's arm. And as for those legs. I've seen better-looking legs on a bridge table. Benny with those vegetarian gams!

HARRY   Has Jack got vegetarian legs, Fred?

ALLEN   Has he? Where there should be a calf, Benny's got aspic. At a cannibal dinner Benny wouldn't even be on the menu. I'll knock that guy so cold he'll think he's something Admiral Byrd left behind.

PORTLAND   Jack said on his program he saved your life in vaudeville.

ALLEN   Nobody saved my life in vaudeville. I died everywhere. The first time I met Benny was in Elyria, Ohio. He was doing a monologue with a pig on the stage.

PORTLAND   A pig?

ALLEN   Yes. The pig was there to eat up the stuff the audience threw at Benny. It was in his contract that he had to leave the stage the way he found it. Some weeks he used to use two pigs.

PORTLAND   What kind of an act was Jack doing then, Mr. Allen?

ALLEN   It was one of those acts. It wasn't safe to take a deep breath while he was on. He used to open the act throwing his violin on the stage. Then, if nothing happened, Benny came on.

HARRY   And Jack didn't save your life?

ALLEN   I saved his life. I'll never forget it. Benny was out on the stage in his spangled tights playing the violin. His big number was Pony

Sport

*"Hello, upstream?
You may release the trout now."*

Boy. He just started to play Pony Boy when a man in the front row started to shoot.

HARRY   A Westerner?

ALLEN   No, a music lover. I ran out on the stage in front of Jack. I thought the star running on might save his life. In the excitement Benny stole two bows and I was shot in the chest. They took me to the hospital.

PORTLAND   Is that when Jack gave you the transfusion?

ALLEN   Yes, Portland. They told me in the hospital later. It was the first time at a transfusion the donor ever asked for a receipt for his blood.

HARRY   Did the transfusion help you?

ALLEN   I had a relapse. Then as a result of the Benny transfusion I had anemia for two years. And it affected me in other ways. I couldn't get my hand in my money pocket for months. I found myself window shopping at toupee stores. It was terrible.

HARRY   How do you fight, Fred? Do you come out punching?

ALLEN   Benny'll think he's a time clock, Harry.

"Now, go out there and win!"

HARRY   I hear Benny can take a lot of body punishment.

ALLEN   He's a pan dowdy with skin on. Benny's stomach hangs down like a Jello knapsack. I'll frappe him. Mr. Benny, I am at your service.

The Owl Who Was God

by James Thurber

Once upon a starless midnight there was an owl who sat on the branch of an oak tree. Two ground moles tried to slip quietly by, unnoticed. "You!" said the owl. "Who?" they quavered, in fear and astonishment, for they could not believe it was possible for anyone to see them in that thick darkness. "You two!" said the owl. The moles hurried away and told the other creatures of the field and forest that the owl was the greatest and wisest of all animals because he could see in the dark and because he could answer any question. "I'll see about that," said a secretary bird, and he called on the owl one night when it was again very dark. "How many claws am I holding up?" said the secretary bird, "Two," said the owl, and that was right. "Can you give me another expression for 'that is to say' or 'namely'?" asked the secretary bird. "To wit," said the owl. "Why does a lover call on his love?" asked the secretary bird. "To woo," said the owl.

The secretary bird hastened back to the other creatures and reported that the owl was indeed the greatest and wisest animal in the world because he could see in the dark and because he could answer any question. "Can he see in the daytime, too?" asked a red fox. "Yes," echoed a dormouse and a French poodle. "Can he see in the daytime, too?" All the other creatures laughed loudly at this silly question, and they set upon the red fox and his friends and drove them out of the region. Then they sent a messenger to the owl and asked him to be their leader.

When the owl appeared among the animals it was high noon and the sun was shining brightly. He walked very slowly, which gave him an appearance of great dignity, and he peered about him with large, staring eyes, which gave him an air of tremendous importance. "He's God!" screamed a Plymouth Rock hen. And the others took up the cry "He's God!" So they followed him wherever he went and when be began to bump into things they began to bump into things, too. Finally he came to a concrete highway and he started up the middle of it and all the other creatures followed him. Presently a hawk, who was acting as outrider, observed a truck coming toward them at fifty miles an hour, and he reported to the secretary bird and the secretary bird reported to the owl. "There's danger ahead," said the secretary bird. "To wit?" said the owl. The secretary bird told him. "Aren't you afraid?" he asked. "Who?" said the owl calmly, for he could not see the truck. "He's God!" cried all the creatures again, and they were still crying "He's God!" when the truck hit them and ran them down. Some of the animals were merely injured, but most of them, including the owl, were killed.

Moral: You can fool too many of the people too much of the time.

Song To Be Sung by the Father of Infant Female Children

by Ogden Nash

My heart leaps up when I behold
A rainbow in the sky;
Contrariwise, my blood runs cold
When little boys go by.
For little boys as little boys,
No special hate I carry,
But now and then they grow to men,
And when they do, they marry.
No matter how they tarry,
Eventually they marry.
And, swine among the pearls,
They marry little girls.

Oh, somewhere, somewhere, an infant plays,
With parents who feed and clothe him.
Their lips are sticky with pride and praise,
But I have begun to loathe him.
Yes, I loathe with a loathing shameless
This child who to me is nameless.
This bachelor child in his carriage
Gives never a thought to marriage,
But a person can hardly say knife
Before he will hunt him a wife.

I never see an infant (male),
A-sleeping in the sun,

AL CAPP'S SHMOO

The Human Condition

THE TIMID SOUL

COWBOYS OUT OUR WAY

Without I turn a trifle pale
And think, is he the one?
Oh, first he'll want to crop his curls,
And then he'll want a pony,
And then he'll think of pretty girls
And holy matrimony.
He'll put away his pony,
And sigh for matrimony.
A cat without a mouse
Is he without a spouse.

Oh, somewhere he bubbles bubbles of milk,
And quietly sucks his thumbs.
His cheeks are roses painted on silk,
And his teeth are tucked in his gums.
But alas, the teeth will begin to grow,
And the bubbles will cease to bubble;
Given a score of years or so,
The roses will turn to stubble.
He'll sell a bond, or he'll write a book,
And his eyes will get that acquisitive look,
And raging and ravenous for the kill,
He'll boldly ask for the hand of Jill.
This infant whose middle
Is diapered still
Will want to marry
My daughter Jill.

Oh sweet be his slumber and moist his middle!
My dreams, I fear, are infanticiddle.
A fig for embryo Lohengrins!
I'll open all of his safety pins,
I'll pepper his powder, and salt his bottle,
And give him readings from Aristotle.
Sand for his spinach I'll gladly bring,
And Tabasco sauce for his teething ring,
And an elegant, elegant alligator
To play with in his perambulator.
Then perhaps he'll struggle through fire and water
To marry somebody else's daughter.

Poets

by E. B. White

You read, perhaps, about the man who stole four tires from a car in Norfolk, Virginia, and left a purse and a diamond ring untouched on the front seat, with this note: "Roses are red, violets are blue, we like your jewels but your tires are new." The papers said it was a case of a thief who had a flair for poetry. This is palpable nonsense. It was a case of a poet who was willing to attempt any desperate thing, even larceny, in order to place his poem. Clearly, here was a man who had written something and then had gone up and down in the world seeking the precise situation which would activate his poem. It must have meant long nights and days of wandering before he found a car with jewels lying loose in the front seat and four good tires on the wheels. Poets endure much for the sake of their art.

W. C. Fields vs. Charlie McCarthy

From a radio broadcast featuring Fields, ventriloquist Edgar Bergen and Bergen's dummy, Charlie McCarthy

FIELDS	(FADE IN—SINGING)
	"When you wore a tulip
	And I drank mint julep
	And I got a big red nose."
BERGEN	Why, W. C. Fields!
	(APPLAUSE)
CHARLIE	What an ad for black coffee. Well, if it isn't W.C., the original half-man half-nose.
FIELDS	Well, Charlie McCarthy. The woodpecker's pin-up boy. Charles, I hear you got married and raised yourself a cord of kids.
CHARLIE	I fear that isn't quite true, sir.
FIELDS	You fear. . . . Anything I hate is a polite kid.
BERGEN	Bill, it's good to see you again. How true that old proverb is, "Old friends, like old wines, are best."

THE INVENTIONS OF RUBE GOLDBERG

NO MORE CROWDED DANCE FLOORS —

WHEN FLOOR-HOGS CRUSH YOU AGAINST WALL, YOUR HEAD SQUEEZES BULB (A), EXPELLING LAUGHING GAS (B), CAUSING HYENA (C) TO VIBRATE WITH LAUGHTER - THUMB (D) PRESSES ON SPONGE (E) AND WATER (F) TURNS WATER WHEEL (G), CAUSING CORD (H) TO PULL DOWN SHADE (I), EXPOSING SIGN READING SMALL POX, AND CLEARING FLOOR FOR YOUR PLEASURE.

SMALL POX

RUBE GOLDBERG

With the Troops

SAD SACK

The Enemy

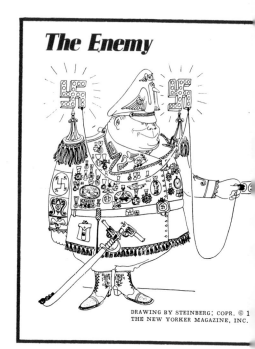

LIFE'S DARKEST MOMENT . . . by Webster

FISHING NEWS FROM HOME

CHARLIE	Mr. Fields, is that your nose, or are you eating a tomato?
FIELDS	Very good, my little chum. You know, Charles, many's the time I've wished you could be here to fill a terrible vacancy.
CHARLIE	In your heart?
FIELDS	No. In my fireplace.
BERGEN	Mr. Fields, what does make your nose so red?
FIELDS	Edgar, my scarlet proboscis is a result of an unfortunate accident in my youth.
CHARLIE	What did you do, fall off a wagon?
FIELDS	Very funny. Tell me, Charles, is it true your father was a gate-leg table?
CHARLIE	If it is—your father was under it.
FIELDS	Why, you stunted spruce—I'll throw a Japanese beetle on you.
CHARLIE	Why, you bar fly—I'll stick a wick in your mouth and use you for an alcohol lamp.
FIELDS	Yes . . . Well, the stuff is really hard to get nowadays.
BERGEN	Well, you see, Bill, alcohol is very important to the war. They're using it in ammunition.
FIELDS	Well, praise the Lord and pass the ammunition.
BERGEN	I just read where there are two ounces of alcohol in a bullet and ten ounces of alcohol in a hand grenade.
FIELDS	Well, shake hands with an old blockbuster.

like them squeezed. Which reminds me, somebody get me a sedative with an olive in it.

FIELDS	Yes indeed, Edgar . . . especially the wine.
BERGEN	Bill, I was going to bring you a basket of fruit, but I decided to ask you what you liked best and have it sent out.
FIELDS	Brandied peaches are very nourishing—I

CHARLIE	I have no sympathy for a man who's intoxicated all the time.
FIELDS	A man who's intoxicated all the time doesn't need sympathy.
BERGEN	Gentlemen, please!
FIELDS	One more crack out of you, Charlie, and I'll nail some runners on your stomach and use you for a sled.
CHARLIE	Oh, you *sleigh* me.
FIELDS	Charles, if you were sawdust on a bar-room floor I'd walk eight blocks for a chocolate soda. I've never had a kid irritate me so much since the day I was born.
CHARLIE	You weren't born . . . You were squeezed out of a bar rag.

If Grant Had Been Drinking at Appomattox

by James Thurber

The morning of the ninth of April, 1865, dawned beautifully. General Meade was up with the first streaks of crimson in the eastern sky. General Hooker and General Burnside were up, and had breakfasted, by a quarter after eight. The day continued beautiful. It drew on toward eleven o'clock. General Ulysses S. Grant was still not up. He was asleep in his famous old navy hammock, swung high above the floor of his headquarters' bedroom. Headquarters was distressingly disarranged: papers were strewn on the floor; confidential notes from spies scurried here and there in the breeze from an open window; the dregs of an overturned bottle of wine flowed pinkly across an important military map.

Corporal Shultz, of the Sixty-fifth Ohio Volunteer Infantry, aide to General Grant, came into the outer room, looked around him, and sighed. He entered the bedroom and shook the General's hammock roughly. General Ulysses S. Grant opened one eye.

"Pardon, sir," said Corporal Shultz, "but this is the day of surrender. You ought to be up, sir."

"Don't swing me," said Grant, sharply, for his aide was making the hammock sway gently. "I feel terrible," he added, and he turned over and closed his eye again.

"General Lee will be here any minute now," said the Corporal firmly, swinging the hammock again.

"Will you cut that out?" roared Grant. "D'ya want to make me sick, or what?" Shultz clicked his heels and saluted. "What's he coming here for?" asked the General.

"This is the day of surrender, sir," said Shultz. Grant grunted bitterly.

"Three hundred and fifty generals in the Northern armies," said Grant, "and he has to come to *me* about this. What time is it?"

"You're the Commander-in-Chief, that's why," said Corporal Shultz. "It's eleven twenty-five, sir."

"Don't be crazy," said Grant. "Lincoln is the Commander-in-Chief. Nobody in the history of the world ever surrendered before lunch. Doesn't he know that an

The Home Front

"We feel very fortunate that any fowl at all came in."

© SYD HOFF

"Who, me?"

"I don't see, Wilthington, how you can be so concerned about the war, while we are all being threatened by the possibility of a fourth term!"

army surrenders on its stomach?" He pulled a blanket up over his head and settled himself again.

"The generals of the Confederacy will be here any minute now," said the Corporal. "You really ought to be up, sir."

Grant stretched his arms above his head and yawned.

"All right, all right," he said. He rose to a sitting position and stared about the room. "This place looks awful," he growled.

"You must have had quite a time of it last night, sir," ventured Shultz.

"Yeh," said General Grant, looking around for his clothes. "I was wrassling some general. Some general with a beard."

Shultz helped the commander of the Northern armies in the field to find his clothes.

"Where's my other sock?" demanded Grant. Shultz began to look around for it. The General walked uncertainly to a table and poured a drink from a bottle.

"I don't think it wise to drink, sir," said Shultz.

"Nev' mind about me," said Grant, helping himself to a second, "I can take it or let it alone. Didn' ya ever hear the story about the fella went to Lincoln to complain about me drinking too much? 'So-and-So says Grant drinks too much,' this fella said. 'So-and-So is a fool,'

"Aren't you just crazy about these USO blind-date parties?"

said Lincoln. So this fella went to What's-His-Name and told him what Lincoln said and he came roarin' to Lincoln about it. 'Did you tell So-and-So I was a fool?' he said. 'No,' said Lincoln, 'I thought he knew it.'" The General smiled, reminiscently, and had another drink. "*That's* how I stand with Lincoln," he said, proudly.

The soft thudding sound of horses' hooves came through the open window. Shultz hurriedly walked over and looked out.

"Hoof steps," said Grant, with a curious chortle.

"It is General Lee and his staff," said Shultz.

"Show him in," said the General, taking another drink. "And see what the boys in the back room will have."

Shultz walked smartly over to the door, opened it, saluted, and stood aside. General Lee, dignified against the blue of the April sky, magnificent in his dress uniform, stood for a moment framed in the doorway. He walked in, followed by his staff. They bowed, and stood silent. General Grant stared at them. He only had one boot on and his jacket was unbuttoned.

"I know who you are," said Grant. "You're Robert Browning, the poet."

"This is General Robert E. Lee," said one of his staff, coldly.

"Oh," said Grant. "I thought he was Robert Browning He certainly looks like Robert Browning. There was a poet for you, Lee: Browning. Did ja ever read 'How They Brought the Good News from Ghent to Aix'? Up Derek, to saddle, up Derek, away; up Dunder, up Blitzen, up Prancer, up Dancer, up Bouncer, up Vixen, up——"

"Shall we proceed at once to the matter in hand?" asked General Lee, his eyes disdainfully taking in the disordered room.

"Some of the boys was wrassling here last night," explained Grant. "I threw Sherman, or some general a whole lot like Sherman. It was pretty dark." He handed a bottle of Scotch to the commanding officer of the Southern armies, who stood holding it, in amazement and discomfiture. "Get a glass, somebody," said Grant, looking straight at General Longstreet. "Didn't I meet you at Cold Harbor?" he asked. General Longstreet did not answer.

"I should like to have this over with as soon as possible," said Lee. Grant looked vaguely at Shultz, who walked up close to him, frowning.

"The surrender, sir, the surrender," said Corporal Shultz in a whisper.

"Oh sure, sure," said Grant. He took another drink. "All right," he said. "Here we go." Slowly, sadly, he unbuckled his sword. Then he handed it to the astonished Lee. "There you are, General," said Grant. "We dam' near licked you. If I'd been feeling better we *would* of licked you."

The Veteran

"*How's it feel to be a free man, Willie?*"

"*. . . and as you leave these tranquil, ivied walls to face the stern realities of life . . .*"

Nonpareil

DRAWING BY PETER ARNO; COPR. © 1943
THE NEW YORKER MAGAZINE, INC.

Censorship

by E. B. White

We are delighted with the recent censorship ruling in the matter of motion-picture harems. Some scenes in a Paramount picture now in production are set in a harem, and after careful deliberation the censors have decided to allow this type of polyform allure *provided* the boudoir does not contain the sultan. The girls can mill about among the pillows, back and side having gone bare, but no male eye must gaze upon them—save, of course, yours, lucky reader. This harem-but-no-sultan decision belongs in the truly great body of opinion interpreting the American moral law. It takes its place alongside the celebrated 1939 ruling on the exposure of female breasts in the Flushing World of Tomorrow, which provided that one breast could be presented publicly but not two, and thereby satisfied the two seemingly irreconcilable groups: the art-lovers, who demanded breasts but were willing to admit that if you'd seen one you'd seen them both, and the decency clique, who held out for concealment but were agreed that the fact of concealing one breast established the essential reticence of the owner and thereby covered the whole

DRAWING BY CHAS. ADDAMS; COPR. © 1940, 1968
THE NEW YORKER MAGAZINE, INC.

situation, or chest. That subtle and far-reaching ruling carried the Fair, as we know, safely through two difficult seasons, and we imagine that the aseptic harem will do as much for Hollywood.

Frank & the Bird

by Paul O'Neil

Pearl River, N.Y., is only 22 miles from Times Square, but it is fully as quiet—or was until last week—as Moccasin, Mont., Husband, Pa., or Clam, Va. Last week, as everyone in Pearl River will remember ("You can say that again, Mac")—as everyone in Pearl River will remember, Frank Perkins, a peaceful, pippin-faced youth of 21, went crow-hunting along the brackish banks of the Hackensack River.

Hardly had he gotten out of his car, .22 rifle in hand, when he spotted a crow. The crow flew. Frank followed, patiently afoot, past fallow fields, thin thickets, ragged coverts and other unfortunate evidences of that dilapidated state into which nature habitually falls in winter. The crow stopped occasionally, but it covered about half a mile, as an erratic crow flies, before it roosted invitingly in a tree just beyond a ramshackle wooden building. Frank crossed a mossy log over a creek and got within 100 feet of his quarry. Balancing there, he drew a bead and fired.

Balls of Fire. At once the building blew up in his face. Five other buildings blew up too; one horrible, earsplitting crash followed another. The sky was lost in smoke, balls of fire whanged in all directions, and the surrounding woodland was magically garnished by endless streamers of colored paper. Frank didn't know what to think. Not until hours later did he learn that the wandering crow had lured him to the plant of the Barnabas Fireworks Co.

He fell backwards off the log into the mud, fled across the creek, dropped his rifle, yanked off his shoes, dived into the Hackensack River and swam it like a beaver heading for a woodyard. As he emerged dripping, on the other side, he thought, dazedly, that he ought to call the fire department. This was unnecessary. Windows had been broken and the population jolted for miles around; the fire departments of Pearl River, Sparkill, Orangeburg, Park Ridge, Northvale and Montvale were already on their way. So were assorted ambulances and police cars.

The Question. Few of them reached the scene. Thousands of householders—all of whom concluded that an atomic bomb had gone off, and all of whom seemed possessed with the idea of getting radioactive as soon as possible—leaped into their cars and soon clogged the roads into impassibility. Then they jumped out and hustled across fields toward the smoke.

As it turned out, there was little to see. The buildings had simply vanished. All the fireworks employees had left 20 minutes before the explosion, and there were no casualties. The big sensation of the whole affair was Frank, who dutifully dragged himself to the police and told all. But Frank didn't enjoy it. Because of the confusion, it took him hours to get home (where he found the windows broken and had two quick belts of whiskey). As a result of his confusion, he was fined $250 for shooting in a forbidden zone. But worst of all was The Question, which he expected to hear until he died.

"Frank," everyone asked, "Frank—what happened to the crow, Frank?"

"People are no damn good."

The Men Who Made the Music:
Artie Shaw

On the evening of November 15, 1939, Artie Shaw might reasonably have felt that, after fifteen years of ferocious effort, he had it made. Here he was at Manhattan's swank Cafe Rouge, leading the best big band he had ever fronted, a band that was one of the best in the business. He was an acknowledged virtuoso clarinetist with a highly personal style; some musicians admired him for an instrumental technique they considered more facile than Benny Goodman's; a vast public simply enjoyed his silken, romantic tones. He was darkly, dashingly handsome, had already been married twice and was making upwards of $250,000 a year.

Yet Shaw was in a snappish mood that night. Trumpeter Bernie Privin recalls: "An elderly woman asked Shaw to play a tango, maybe it was a rhumba. He said, 'Lady, you're in the wrong room.'" A little later he walked off the bandstand and did not return. He told a few of the sidemen after the band had finished the evening without him that he was sick and was quitting for good, and with that he drove off to Mexico, not even bothering to say good-by to the rest of the band. "He said not a goddamned thing to us," says violinist-arranger Jerry Gray. "Shaw should've faced us."

Shaw had worked the band hard. "He got on everybody's back," says trombonist Harry Rodgers. He had refused Privin two weeks off to get married because he felt a substitute trumpeter could not easily learn the band's complicated "book." The band was just beginning to enjoy prosperity. "We *did* work for peanuts trying to get there," says Rodgers. "I started in 1937. Shaw quit in 1939. That's two years of knocking around the road for one good year." Few of the sidemen soon got jobs as good as they had had with Shaw. Privin's salary dropped from $125 a week to $50. And, says Privin, "Shaw left a $700 bill [at the hotel]. It was deducted from our salaries." But some of his sidemen agreed with the *New York Times* writer who called Shaw's gesture "a beautifully incautious burning of all his bridges behind him." The sidemen understood perhaps better than anyone else that Shaw was a complex and tormented man whose behavior was not easily confined, even to the rather elastic standards of musicians. They often quit good jobs themselves for reasons an outsider would find trivial if not totally incomprehensible. Tommy Dorsey had abandoned the Dorsey Brothers band in 1935 after a disagreement on tempo.

"A lot of us kinda agreed with him," says Rodgers. "We admired his nerve. As a musician, you get annoyed all the time, but you cover up, if you do it for a living."

For saxophonist Les Robinson, "It was like the end of the world. I damn near cried. Maybe I did cry. The band was really big, and for it to break up was as if the [Los Angeles football] Rams suddenly disbanded. It was headlines. All of the leaders came in like vultures, you know, 'I'll take him . . . I'll take him.'" Yet Robinson and others returned again and again to play in later Shaw bands. They respected Shaw as a musician and with him they felt they were at the top.

Backed by a small group—a rhythm section and a string quartet—Artie Shaw scored a hit at a swing concert in New York's Imperial Theater on May 24, 1936 with his quiet *Interlude in B Flat*. He was soon flooded with job offers.

"When he walked away," says guitarist Al Avola, recalling that night at the Cafe Rouge, "he took the band with him. We tried. We played the same music and it was swinging. But something was missing. He was the band."

No Swing Era leader ever jumped clear out of the band business, as Shaw eventually did, from the altitude Shaw had reached before he quit. The evidence of his success is on the popularity charts and on some four hundred recordings, which preserve not only the rich and resonant sound of his clarinet but the evidence of his originality as a composer and his skill and taste in selecting arrangements, combining instrumental voices and creating such distinctive sounds as those of his sparkling little Gramercy Five.

Shaw won almost entirely on his own the laurels he later discarded. His mother, for some reason, always called him "Arthur," but he was formally named Abraham Isaac Arshawsky when he was born on May 23, 1910. He spent his first seven years on New York's Lower East Side. Then his parents moved to New Haven, Connecticut, after their dressmaking business failed. At school, the shy little newcomer was teased and bullied. In his autobiography, *The Trouble with Cinderella*, he remembers the period as one of brutal anti-Semitic persecution.

Artie Arshawsky retreated to a world of books and music. Piano lessons bored him, but at Poli's Palace, a vaudeville theater, he sat entranced watching a young man in a blue-and-white striped blazer play *Dreamy Melody* on a gleaming saxophone with mother-of-pearl keys. Shaw had caught the vision that launched so many Swing Era stars: music could be an escape to glamorous living. Shaw worked all summer in a delicatessen to earn the forty dollars he spent on a second-hand C-melody sax. Working by himself, he mastered several popular tunes and entered an amateur contest in a little neighborhood theater. Although the pit pianist and the young saxophonist started in different keys "and never did manage to get together until practically the very end," Shaw won the five-dollar first prize with a rendition of *Charley My Boy*.

After that Shaw practiced up to seven hours a day until "my teeth ached and the inside of my lower lip was ragged and cut from the constant pressure of the mouthpiece and reed." He got little encouragement at home. "Who needs it?" said his father of the instrument he always called a "blower." But there was that five-dollar prize, so Shaw's parents let him keep blowing, although his father at about this time left home, never to return.

Shaw got a few gigs with amateur groups, then an audition with a local dance band led by Johnny Cavallaro. Shaw got numbly through one number which he had previously memorized. "You'll have to learn to read," said Cavallaro. In just one month Shaw became a competent sight reader, won a steady job in the reed section and became one of very few fifteen-year-old American boys who in 1925 were earning thirty to forty dollars a week. He also changed his name to Arthur Shaw.

The band got a summer date playing at a lakeside lodge at Bantam Lake near Litchfield, Connecticut. The sidemen passed one Sunday afternoon drinking boilermakers, shots of whiskey with beer chasers. Shaw was a novice drinker but determined to hold his own. He came groggily awake that evening. It was nearly time for the band to start playing for a dance. Shaw raced to the bandstand. The lights came up and there he sat, still in a red bathing suit. Cavallaro, swinging his banjo like a mace, chased Shaw out of the hall and down to the lake. While Shaw sat trembling and out of reach in a rowboat, Cavallaro, on the dock, "raved on like a crazy man" but eventually gave up and "went cursing back to the ballroom."

The next time he saw Shaw, Cavallaro fired him. Shaw joined a band made up of inexperienced youngsters. It broke up in Kentucky, leaving him stranded there. Another traveling band picked him up and sustained him until he could save up for his fare back to New Haven. By then Cavallaro had cooled off enough to offer Shaw a job with the band for a winter engagement in Miami. The job required a saxophonist who could double on clarinet. Shaw failed to mention that he had never played a clarinet. Convinced, as always, that he could learn anything he wanted to, he bought a clarinet and practiced the unfamiliar instrument all the way to Miami. He learned to produce "a few heart-rending squeaks and squeals." The first rehearsal convinced Cavallaro that he still lacked a clarinetist. He could try to make a clarinetist out of Shaw or he could, as union rules required, pay Shaw's fare home and import somebody else. "One of the nicest things he called me," Shaw recalls, "was a 'dirty little no-good son-of-a-bitch.'" He kept Shaw, who soon learned enough clarinet to get by and who improved enough as a musician to land a $125-a-week job back in New Haven with the Olympia Theater pit band.

Arranging from the ground up

Shaw moved on to a year's contract with Joe Cantor, then leading a house band at a Chinese restaurant in Cleveland. At sixteen, Shaw tried his first arrangement. Lacking even enough know-how to use an arranger's vertical score sheet, he spent an evening crawling around the floor writing an arrangement of *Wabash Blues* for first one instrument and then another, guessing at how the whole would sound when put together. It sounded awful at the first rehearsal. Some parts were completely unplayable. But the arrangement was basically sound, and the sidemen eventually cobbled together a workable version.

As always, Shaw learned fast. At the end of his year with Cantor he moved on to Austin Wylie's Orchestra, then Cleveland's top name band, and began turning out arrangements for Wylie at a tremendous pace. Shaw was now in his late teens and living on his nerves. He drove himself into insomnia and during some of his sleepless hours entered a contest being run by a Cleveland newspaper. Each contestant was supposed to submit an essay and a title for a song celebrating Cleveland's selection as the site of the National Air Races. Artie's essay and his song title, *Song of the Skies*, won first prize—an all-expense air trip to Hollywood.

Artie got a leave of absence from Wylie in the summer of 1929 and went to Hollywood where he ran across some old friends, trumpeter Charlie Trotta and saxophonist Tony Pestritto (later Pastor), who were playing in Irving Aaronson's band at the Roosevelt Hotel. Shaw went there to hear the band and to get a look at Hollywood high life. He sat on a balcony gazing enraptured at such divinities as Jean Harlow, Joan Crawford and Charlie Chaplin. He listened with less rapture to Irving Aaronson and his Commanders.

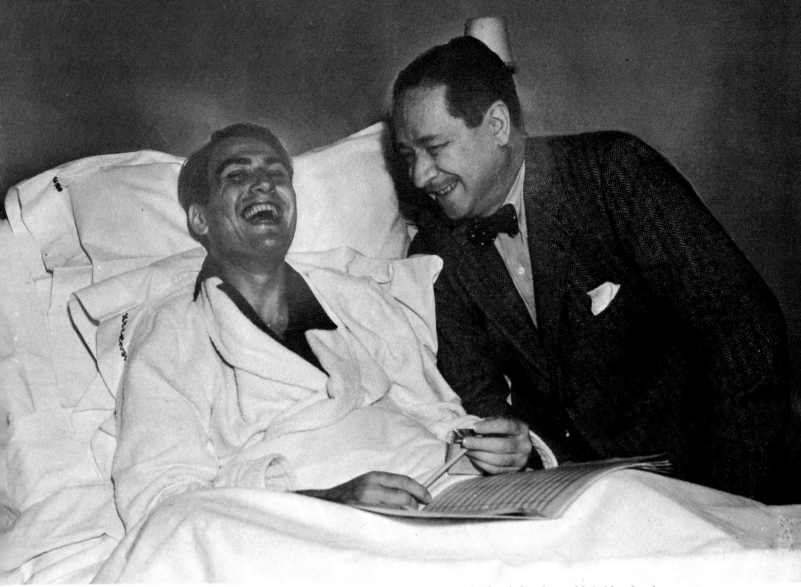

In 1939 a blood disease nearly killed Shaw and put him in a Los Angeles hospital. Writer-comic Robert Benchley, then appearing with Shaw's band on Old Gold radio show, visits the patient who, by coincidence, displays sponsor's product.

His friends had offered to get Shaw into the Aaronson band, but Shaw was not sure he wanted to leave Wylie. Aaronson was nationally famous, but the band struck the critical Shaw as corny and less competent than Wylie's.

On the other hand, Shaw was bored to death with his job and with Cleveland. One winter night, just to get away from the city for a while, he drove in a blizzard to Akron and sat all night in a hotel lobby. From insomnia, he swung toward coma. He would sink into trances so deep that his friend Claude Thornhill, then pianist with the Wylie band, and Wylie himself were wearing themselves out trying to shake Shaw into some semblance of consciousness for afternoon performances.

The Aaronson band came to Cleveland. Aaronson listened to Shaw playing with the Wylie band and made him an offer. After further agonizing indecision, Shaw joined Aaronson and returned to Hollywood and the Roosevelt Hotel. He was immediately dissatisfied to find that everybody in the band except himself had some specialty number like a song-and-dance bit. Infuriated at having to sit unnoticed on the bandstand while others got the spotlight, Shaw wrote an arrangement of *Dinah* with a vocal chorus for himself. Mega-phone in hand, he used to step out in front of the band and warble. Aaronson, busy leading the band, apparently paid little attention at first to Shaw's vocal solo. But one night Aaronson happened to catch Shaw's act from the other end of the Roosevelt's Blossom Room while trombonist Red Stanley was substituting as leader. "Jesus Christ!" said Aaronson, "that kid's got the personality of a dead *lox!*"

Shaw stopped singing and resumed playing. Aaronson's band never rose to Shaw's standards, but Artie enjoyed making good money and visiting interesting places like Chicago. There, after an evening of grinding out pop tunes with Aaronson at the Granada Cafe, Shaw could seek out musicians he respected. He listened to Louis Armstrong's little combo at the Sunset Cafe. He sat in with the big Earl Hines band at the Grand Terrace. Once, after hours, he sat in with a band which was playing, mostly for the fun of playing, at a dance marathon. Shaw listened in fascination to some of the great Chicago jazz stylists of the day. Jess Stacy and Joe Sullivan each took a turn at the piano. Floyd O'Brien's trombone wandered around the melody, starting off time after time in directions which sounded like mistakes. "After a while," Shaw later wrote, "you began to get the idea that

Chief Petty Officer Shaw leads Navy Band 501 in a concert for the crews of two U.S. warships somewhere in the South Pacific during August 1943. Incessant island-hopping under combat conditions left Shaw and his men near collapse.

this guy not only wasn't making any mistakes at all, but had complete control over his horn." Frank Teschemacher's clarinet seemed to Shaw to be fumbling for "some phrase you couldn't quite see the beginning or end of (or, for that matter, the reason for in the first place)" but which in the end, and in a highly personal way, made subtle musical sense.

Nobody with Shaw's musical acumen could have failed to learn from these artists something of the beat and the spirit of the jazz which was becoming swing. Shaw learned. He also suddenly became interested in classical music and began buying Stravinsky recordings like *The Firebird Suite* and *Sacre du Printemps*. His horizons expanded. At the same time came a stroke of bad luck: he was driving down a Manhattan street when he struck a pedestrian who had stepped in front of his car and who died almost instantly. The accident was clearly unavoidable. Manslaughter charges against Shaw were dropped, but he brooded about the affair and about the civil suit for damages which arose from it. The suit kept him tied to New York after the Aaronson band left, and union rules kept him from working in New York for six months.

Gloomy and unemployed, Shaw drifted to Harlem and spent his nights listening to some of the world's best jazz and making friends with the great stride pianist Willie ("The Lion") Smith, then playing at Pod's and Jerry's, a speakeasy on West 133rd Street. First he just listened, then he sat in

with Willie. The Lion is chary with accolades, but finally he said of Shaw: "My boy Artie was a good student, and the Lion was proud of him when we went out to jam after finishing our nightly stint at P.'s and J.'s." Shaw says that with the black jazzmen of Harlem he felt a relationship warmer than any he had ever enjoyed with men his own color.

The crash of 1929 added to Shaw's difficulties. Even with a union card, he found jobs scarce. "I felt . . . like a wild animal trapped in a snare and ready to gnaw its own leg off to gain freedom," he says in a typical passage from his book. Before he actually had to gnaw off a leg, he got a job as a CBS studio musician. He suffered impatiently through the usual idiocies of studio work, like the dictum of the sponsor who cut out a Shaw clarinet solo because he was paying for thirty-five musicians and wanted to hear all thirty-five all the time. Yet this studio period was not a complete drag for Shaw. He made four fine recordings for Columbia in October 1934 with Red Norvo and his Swing Septet; Shaw has a particularly lovely, warm passage in *I Surrender Dear*.

Studio work paid well enough to permit Shaw to buy a dilapidated house on twenty-five weedy acres in Bucks County, Pennsylvania, where he retired from music and spent a year cutting and selling firewood and writing and tearing up a novel about his former roommate, the legendary jazz cornetist Bix Beiderbecke.

Shaw returned to New York in 1936 to find jobs scarce

Chicago autograph-seekers engulf a distraught-looking Shaw on December 11, 1944 following one of his first postwar concerts. After hospitalization and discharge from the Navy, he had formed a new band and embarked on psychoanalysis.

again. "I remember my first day in town," he wrote later. "From ten until two I toured the studios and offices. All I got was the story I shouldn't have quit the business cold when it was paying me good money. From two until four I sat on a park bench getting more and more panicky. All I knew was music. If I couldn't sell that what could I sell?"

That same day he got an offer of a spot in a "Swing Music Concert" being organized by Joe Helbock, proprietor of the Onyx Club. Helbock was well qualified to assemble a contingent of swing musicians. Most of them had been coming to his 52nd Street joint since the day it opened for business as a speakeasy in 1930. Tommy Dorsey used to head for the jam session at the Onyx every evening after playing at the Glen Island Casino. Mike Riley and Eddy Farley introduced at the Onyx the Swing Era anthem which made them famous, *The Music Goes 'Round and Around*. Joe Sullivan was the club's house pianist for a while, and Stuff Smith's band made its New York debut there.

The program Helbock arranged for the concert at New York's Imperial Theater included groups led by Joe Venuti, Wingy Manone, Bob Crosby, Red Norvo, Stuff Smith,

Shaw *(center)* testifies in 1953 before the House Un-American Activities Committee *(foreground)*; its chairman praised his frank account of his brief brush with U.S. Communists.

Shaw was a veteran of two marriages, an annulment and a divorce when he eloped with 19-year-old Lana Turner (*left*) in February 1940. Their marriage lasted less than a year. In 1942 he married composer Jerome Kern's daughter Elizabeth (*center*). They had a son before parting in 1944. He married Ava Gardner (*right*) in 1945, divorced her in 1946.

Bunny Berigan, Tommy Dorsey, Adrian Rollini, Louis Armstrong and Red Nichols. Paul Whiteman loaned nine of his men, including Jack and Charlie Teagarden and Frankie Trumbauer. Glen Gray and the Casa Loma Orchestra had the closing spot on the bill.

Star sidemen were thick on the ground, among them Joe Marsala, Tony Sbarbaro, Jonah Jones, Cozy Cole, Eddie Condon, Joe Bushkin, Max Kaminsky, Bud Freeman, Davey Tough, Paul Barbarin, Pops Foster, Luis Russell, Toots Mondello and Miff Mole.

Third on the program was "Arthur Shaw's String Swing Ensemble." The ensemble was a rhythm section combined with a string quartet which Shaw had organized a few days before the concert. Shrewdly anticipating a program heavy with hot and brassy music, Shaw wrote for his group, in about an hour, a quiet but swinging chamber jazz piece, *Interlude in B Flat.*

An interlude that stopped the show

The Wingy Manone band finished its set with a tremendous finale. Shaw led his odd little combo onstage. "My knees were knocking together like a pair of castanets," he says. When his ensemble finished its piece, Shaw had only one thought—to get offstage. Joe Helbock grabbed him. "That was *great*, Art—listen to them out there!" In response to continuing applause, Helbock shoved Shaw back onstage. The group repeated *Interlude*, the only number it had had time to master. More applause. "Artie's one number," wrote jazz critic Leonard Feather, "broke up the show."

A couple of months later Art Shaw and his Orchestra opened at New York's Hotel Lexington with the group from the Imperial Theater triumph plus four horns. The band lasted about six months, but for such a short-lived outfit it left a surprisingly complete testament—the thirty sides it recorded for Brunswick. Peg La Centra's wistful, reedy voice enhances the charm of *You're Giving Me a Song and a Dance* and *There's Something in the Air*. In instrumentals like *Thou Swell*, *Sobbing Blues* and *Copenhagen*, the band presents a relaxed kind of swing combining the jazz feeling of its basically Dixieland instrumentation with the soft mood of its string quartet.

Unfortunately, the band was something less than a smash at the Lexington, at the French Casino, at the Paramount Theater and, finally, on the road. The Rockwell-O'Keefe agency had trouble getting further bookings and the band folded.

"There was no room for the sort of musical subtleties I was trying to create with this atypical little band," Shaw wrote later. "A new fad swept the nation. If a band couldn't play good music, it could always call itself a 'swing band' and play *loud* music instead."

To meet the challenge of loud competition, Shaw decided to form "the loudest band in the whole goddam world." The result was Art Shaw and his New Music, a fourteen-piece group without strings but including some top musicians like trumpeter John Best, saxophonists Tony Pastor and Les Robinson, trombonist George Arus, guitarist Al Avola and drummer Cliff Leeman.

"We hit the road in an old truck we had bought from Tommy Dorsey," Shaw later recalled. "It had Tommy's name painted on both sides, weatherbeaten but legible. Until we had enough money to pay for repainting the body, we were stopped three times for having stolen it. A cop in Boston arrested our Negro driver and tossed him in the can. He had heard Tommy Dorsey broadcasting from New York an hour before. We left our driver in jail, the truck in the police yard, and went on to our next stand by bus."

The old truck and a couple of second-hand cars Shaw

picked up later carried the band through two years of one-nighters "in a stuffy hall or an ex-barn from which the cows had only recently been evicted." Over the misgivings of some of his sidemen, Shaw avoided pop tunes and stuck to a repertory of musical-comedy songs and some of his own originals. "I argued that dancers would go for good arrangements of songs old or new."

By early 1938 people were starting to go for Shaw's music. The band got a few broadcasts and then in March opened at Boston's Roseland State Ballroom, owned by Si Shribman who also arranged a series of college engagements. Trumpeter Max Kaminsky remembers alternating with Tommy Dorsey's band at a Dartmouth prom. Dorsey opened with his smooth and gentle theme, *I'm Gettin' Sentimental Over You*. Then Shaw's band came on with the wild and eerie *Nightmare*. The Dartmouth gym exploded in applause, as Kaminsky remembers it. "We actually blew Tommy off the stand. He was a man who was always mad about something, but that night he was so burned up that he grabbed his horn and stalked off the stand."

Shaw recalls that after his band's first number some Dorsey men told him, "Man, you scared us. These guys of yours come on like savages."

In 1937 Shaw hired a new girl singer, Billie Holiday, who was already well known for the records she had made, some of them with a band which included Artie Shaw. As one of the few white bandleaders of the time whose band included a Negro, Shaw made Billie better known in some unexpected places. "Artie was a guy who never thought in terms of white and colored," Billie wrote later. " 'I can take care of the situation,' was his answer." The combative Shaw probably enjoyed the inevitable confrontations. Billie remembered how he swept her into the biggest hotel in a small Kentucky town by having eight band members escort her to the desk "like it was as natural as breathing. I think the man at the desk figured it couldn't be true what he thought he saw, and I couldn't be Negro or nobody would act like that. I think they thought I was Spanish or something, so they gave me a nice room and no back talk."

Fifteen feet apart for racial propriety

Four years later, prejudice was still so strong that Shaw was told he could include the black trumpeter-vocalist Hot Lips Page on a Southwest tour only if Page sat no less than fifteen feet away from the nearest white sideman. "I told them to shove it," is the way Shaw remembers canceling the tour.

About the same time he hired Billie Holiday, Shaw had shifted from the Brunswick label to RCA's Bluebird, and in July 1938 the band cut its first six Bluebird sides, including *Any Old Time*, one of the few recorded examples of the splendid blend achieved by Artie's clarinet and Billie's voice. ("Nobody would let me record her," he said recently. "People were uptight about that stuff then.") Shaw thought the biggest hit in the series would be *Indian Love Call* with Tony Pastor singing in the style of Louis Armstrong. But it was Shaw's lilting version of *Begin the Beguine*, on the other side of the record, that zoomed him to the top.

In January 1939 Shaw was packing the jitterbugs into the Blue Room of New York's Lincoln Hotel in such numbers that he was featured in one of the *Life Goes to a Party* series. The story noted that Shaw had beaten out Benny Goodman in the "best band" division of *Down Beat's* annual poll. Shaw, said LIFE, "is now growing rich" but "still insists wistfully that his clarinet and strings were a swell combination."

Shaw was indeed getting rich. Suddenly he was netting up to $30,000 a week from record sales, personal appearances and his weekly Old Gold radio show and was wonder-

Kathleen Winsor *(left)*, author of the sexy best-seller, *Forever Amber*, became the sixth Mrs. Shaw in 1946. They were divorced in 1948. Doris Dowling was Shaw's fiancee when this 1951 picture *(center)* was taken. They were married in 1952, had a son, and were divorced in 1956. Shaw's present wife, actress Evelyn Keyes *(right)*, married him in 1957.

ing, "What the hell could there be about *anyone* that would make him worth that much-money?" Shaw had defeated adversity, but success did him in. While the band was playing at the Palomar Ballroom in Los Angeles and also working in an MGM movie, Shaw contracted a rare blood disease which nearly killed him and diminished his interest in his band. "You can keep it," he told Tony Pastor and Jerry Gray, who had been holding the band together during his illness.

Shaw recovered enough interest to continue leading the band but complained about needing policemen to protect him from "the mob of milling youngsters who wanted nothing more than to pull out my hair for a souvenir." He barely eluded one such mob in Boston which overturned his car. He sneered at his jitterbug following: "If I was made by a bunch of morons, that's just too bad." So many of the "morons" complained about this remark that Shaw and Old Gold parted company. By the time he reached the Cafe Rouge bandstand, Shaw was getting that ready-to-gnaw-off-a-leg feeling again. So, on that memorable evening at the Cafe Rouge, he gnawed off his band and escaped to Mexico. Even there, publicity followed him when he broke a leg in the course of rescuing a young woman from drowning.

A 32-piece comeback

Four months after his great escape Shaw was back in California organizing a thirty-two-piece band with thirteen strings and making some recordings. His dark-toned clarinet made his *Gloomy Sunday* one of the most memorable of the many recorded versions of this lugubrious number. He also recorded *Adios Marquita Linda* and *Frenesi*, tunes he had heard local bands playing in Acapulco. Shaw thought they were folk tunes and was astonished to learn that *Frenesi* had been written by Alberto Dominguez, a contemporary Mexican composer. Dominguez and Shaw both profited handsomely. Shaw's lush and lively arrangement and the growing popularity of Latin-American rhythms made *Frenesi* one of Shaw's biggest hits.

From within his big band Shaw also organized in 1940 the Gramercy Five, which he named after a New York telephone exchange to give it a title more distinctive than just "quintet." With Artie on clarinet, Johnny Guarnieri on harpsichord, Billy Butterfield on trumpet, Jud De Naut on bass and Nick Fatool on drums, the Five recorded eight of the neatest, slickest, most appealing small-group efforts of the Swing Era—stuff like *Special Delivery Stomp* and *Summit Ridge Drive*.

World War II finished the Gramercy Five and the rest of the 1940 Shaw band. After Pearl Harbor, Shaw enlisted in the Navy and was soon a chief petty officer in charge of Navy Band 501. The new CPO had little trouble luring into his twenty-piece outfit such stars as Kaminsky, Thornhill and drummer Davey Tough. Shaw can be very persuasive; musicians respected his abilities, and there was little chance of his abandoning this band in a tantrum. The band spent five rather relaxed months in Honolulu. Shaw, Kaminsky recalls, "was a natural target, in his crisp white chief's uniform, for the bored Navy wives, who all trained their guns on him at every dance we played." But when the band got to Guadalcanal, "The tents in which we were quartered were so riddled by bullets they looked like mosquito net-

ting." After two harrowing years of island-hopping, the band was shipped home in 1943. "By then," Shaw later wrote, "our instruments were being held together by rubber bands and sheer will, having survived any number of air raids and damp spells in foxholes; and the men themselves were for the most part in similarly varying states of dilapidation."

Shaw went into a hospital for a rest and into a year and a half of psychoanalysis, one hour a day, five days a week. He believes the treatment saved him from becoming "an old man with a long gray beard leading a broken-down jazzband in some backwoods dance hall." While exploring his psyche, he also put together another big band and a new Gramercy Five and for a few more years continued to make music—some of it exciting, some of it glossily commercial, all of it produced with taste and distinction, especially the numbers by the new Gramercy Five like *Grabtown Grapple* and *Mysterioso*. As usual, Shaw attracted first-rate sidemen—trumpeters Roy Eldridge and Billy Butterfield, trombonists Jack Jenney and Ray Conniff, guitarist Barney Kessel, baritone saxophonist Chuck Gentry, pianist Dodo Marmarosa. Shaw experimented freely with new sounds, using five saxes, eight woodwinds, twenty-three strings and four rhythm at one recording session. He never adapted, however, to the new sounds of bop. "If somebody else is doing it," he asked, "why should I?"

He carried the fight into the enemy camp, invaded Bop City on Broadway with a forty-piece band and bombarded bop fans with Walton, Debussy, Ravel and Prokofiev for one unrewarding week. Public apathy toward good music, he concluded, "is a Great Wall of China... and we're attacking it with a nail file."

Shaw's interest in "serious" music is keenly professional. He has won critical plaudits for his performances of two clarinet concertos, one by Nicolai Berezowsky and the other, which Shaw commissioned, by Norman Dello Joio. Less comprehensible to some of his musical acquaintances has been his passionate interest in literature. "He never hit the bottle," says a sideman who knew Shaw in his Aaronson days. "But he was always hitting some goddam book, and he was always telling you what was in it, too. We all wished he'd get loaded."

On or off the bandstand, Shaw continued to make headlines with such activities as his eight marriages, six divorces and one annulment. Shaw had a refreshing explanation for his many marriages: "In Hollywood you lived in a goldfish bowl. You had to get married to keep people from watching you all the time." He also, in 1953, explained to the satisfaction of the House Un-American Activities Committee the nature of his brief and disillusioning flirtation with Communism.

Still firm in his belief that he could do anything he set his mind to, Shaw retired in 1950 to run a dairy farm in Pine Plains, New York, and to write his autobiography. An $80,000 federal back-tax claim stimulated Shaw to return

The modishly mustached 1970 Shaw works in his midtown New York office on such projects as his plans for a musical version of F. Scott Fitzgerald's novel, *The Great Gatsby*.

once more to the bandstand to lead a third, and cooler version of the Gramercy Five at Manhattan's Embers. He offered some new Shaw originals like *Lugubrious, Lyric* and *Overdrive* and a new sound he described as "a liquid pastel sound. Sort of chamber music with a beat. Five guys to sound like one instrument." He also lectured his audience for talking too loudly. "Ladies and gentlemen," he said severely, "I'd like to remind you that it's almost axiomatic that music sounds better against silence. Not dead silence— just enough so that we can hear ourselves play."

He did, however, relax his customarily austere bandstand manner enough to cause a fellow musician to remark: "He still don't remind me none of Jesus Christ, but compared to the old Shaw, he's acting a little like St. Francis." The Embers engagement and a subsequent road tour were critically, and presumably financially, successful, but at the end Shaw felt so wrung out that he left both music and the United States. He went to Spain, built a house, and wrote a trio of novellas published under the title of *I Love You, I Hate You,*

Drop Dead! in one of which a poisonous female gets pushed off a cliff. "That was catharsis, writing that," says Shaw. "It was a great relief to me." Shaw returned to America, became a successful movie distributor, took up rifle marksmanship and proved he could hit a target as well as he ever hit a note. He opened a gunsmith and rifle business in Clinton Corners, New York.

Shaw claims he has no nostalgia for the Swing Era. "Everybody's always talking about the good old days," he said recently. "I don't believe in that . . . . If you're going to buy a Ford—you buy a 1970 Ford." He also affects indifference to appraisals of his accomplishments. "I don't care what people think of my work," he once said. "I never did. You either write notes or you don't write notes, and they either get the message or they don't. I don't care."

But about the work itself, no one who ever listened to a Shaw composition or to one of his clarinet solos—light and lyric or dark and brooding—could doubt that he cared about the music.   —CHRIS ALBERTSON

The Men Who Made the Music:
Glen Gray

CURRENT STANDING in *Paramount* BAND POPULARITY VOTE / Get Your Ballot from Ushers and Vote for *Your favorite* /					
GLEN GRAY	59116	BOB CROSBY	39290	LUD GLUSKIN	30364
GUY LOMBARDO	58745	RUSS MORGAN	38161	CLYDE McCOY	29681
FRED WARING	56881	CAB CALLOWAY	36924	ABE LYMAN	29005
BENNY GOODMAN	56702	WILL OSBORNE	36378	GEORGE HALL	28011
SHEP FIELDS	53714	Andre KOSTELANETZ	35014	TOMMY DORSEY	27751
HAL KEMP	48596	TED LEWIS	33296	DUKE ELLINGTON	27196
EDDY DUCHIN	46094	CLYDE LUCAS	32693	LITTLE JACK LITTLE	25868
LOUIS ARMSTRONG	45118	BEN BERNIE	32414	JAN GARBER	25016
RUDY VALLEE	44001	JACK DENNY	32245	ART SHAW	24989
RAY NOBLE	43663	PAUL WHITEMAN	31998	RICHARD HIMBER	23665
PHIL SPITALNY	42742	VINCENT LOPEZ	31743	GEORGE OLSEN	22076
OZZIE NELSON	41834	Enrique MADRIGUERA	31441	JOHNNY GREEN	21214
WAYNE KING	40328	HORACE HEIDT	30697	RED NICHOLS	20772

On New Year's Eve of 1938, Times Square in New York was crammed as usual. At the Paramount Theater (*below*), also as usual, Glen Gray and the Casa Lomans were featured as they had been every Christmas season since 1935 when the Paramount first added name bands to its attractions. At right, Gray stands in the theater's lobby, happily contemplating the top rating given his band by Paramount patrons.

In mid-1935 Willard Alexander of the Music Corporation of America was booking a new band led by a clarinetist named Benny Goodman. Alexander and Goodman had a specific goal: to challenge the nationwide popularity of the Casa Loma Orchestra, booked by the rival Rockwell-O'Keefe organization. It was a large order. Casa Loma's jazz numbers were wowing the college crowd. Its slow and sentimental ballads were hits with people who thought they didn't like "jazz" but enjoyed music above the level of Guy Lombardo. Casa Loma's music introduced thousands of Americans to swing and provided an entree for some of the bands which followed it to the top of the heap.

Casa Loma was no mere precursor, however. It had plenty to say for itself in music that still falls lovingly upon the ear. It had, in Gene Gifford, one of the best arrangers in swing and, in Glen Gray, a monumentally stable leader. It had, over the years, as attractive a roster of sidemen as most of the other big bands. The musicians blew well and were highly ornamental. Casa Loma was the first dance band to appear consistently in white tie and tails and was, throughout its heyday, the best-dressed band in the business. Even its name breathed a hint of the exotic, of faraway mystery.

When Goodman set out to catch Gray's well-tailored coattails, Casa Loma, because of its enormous popularity, was in its second year as the featured band on radio's Camel Caravan and had been hired by New York's Paramount Theater to launch its new policy of having a name band play onstage between film showings. It was traveling thousands of miles a year and was getting up to $2,500 for a college prom date. Its records were selling better than those of most bands.

Most young musicians liked Casa Loma's big band jazz arrangements, the range and complexity of its library, the extent of orchestral coloring it achieved by having sidemen

In high school in Roanoke, Illinois, "Spike" Knoblauch (later Glen Gray) was good for about seven feet in the pole vault.

able to double on several horns. "The bandstand at Bridgeport was open in the back," says former Casa Loma trombonist Pee Wee Hunt, "and the guys all stood behind us and read our music right along with us, to see if we would make any mistakes."

Out in Seattle, young Larry Wagner was blowing trumpet in the Johnny Robinson band and starting to try his hand as an arranger. "We just couldn't wait for the Casa Loma broadcasts," says Larry, "and we'd be darned sure to time our own sets so that we finished in time to hear them." When Larry later became a Casa Loma arranger himself and composer of one of Glen's big hits, *No Name Jive*, he felt like a conqueror of Everest.

Except for musicians, few people knew or cared that the handsome leader had been born Glen Gray Knoblauch and never could get his tempos right or that the band's euphonious name memorialized a defunct Toronto hotel. Nor did they care that Glen Gray was indeed a leader in all but the conducting sense or that his band was the first and one of the very few successful musical cooperatives of the Swing Era. They just thought the music sounded great.

Glen Gray started making music in central Illinois where he was born on June 7, 1900, in the little town of Metamora, second child and only son of Lurdie and Agnes Gray Knoblauch. His father was a piano tuner who played the violin and led a family orchestra whose other members were Glen's Uncle Ed and his aunts Carrie, Margaret and Eva. The orchestra played at social gatherings in the small towns of the region. Glen's father died when Glen was two, but ten years later Glen acquired an affectionate stepfather when his mother married George DeWilde, a coal-mine manager in Roanoke, Illinois, who encouraged Glen and his sister Mabel in all their endeavors.

As his first musical endeavor, Glen picked up a piccolo which was lying around the house, practiced every day and mastered it. The sound business judgment which marked his whole career led him to assess the demand for piccolo players in small Illinois towns. So he switched to clarinet and became a regular performer in the Thursday-night concerts given in the town square by Wilson's Concert Band. Teenage Glen was six feet tall and slim. His friends called him Spike, and he called the first band he organized "Spike's Jazz Orchestra." The five-piece band with Mabel on piano and Glen as director did its best to sound like the Original Dixieland Jazz Band, the white New Orleans outfit whose records were beginning to inspire young musicians all over the United States.

Music became Glen's life. He had ambitions beyond working as a railroad freight handler by day and leading his band at night. He studied at Illinois Wesleyan for one semester and by 1925 was working steadily in Detroit as a saxophone player and music copyist. In his spare time he invested in the stock market and got married. The marriage soon ended, but Glen's investments prospered, then and later. "They didn't play no benefits for Spike," said a friend after his death.

By 1926 Glen was playing most often with the Jean Goldkette Orange Blossoms. The French-born Goldkette was a slim and scholarly former concert pianist who had studied under composer Mikhail Ippolitov-Ivanov at the Moscow Conservatory. He was a musicians' musician and a fine promoter who could attract talented sidemen and display them effectively. Among those who played for him in the mid-'20s were such eminences of jazz as Bix Beiderbecke, the immortal cornetist; Joe Venuti, one of the few great hot violinists; Eddie Lang, a pioneer jazz guitarist; Pee Wee Russell, the inimitable clarinetist, and the Dorsey brothers. Spike Knoblauch, though never in the same league with these stars, was a respected journeyman among them and shared their feeling for good jazz. Goldkette, like Ben Pollack, was one of the pioneers of big band jazz. In his organization Spike learned a lot about running bands and about combining the sounds of many jazzmen into swinging harmony.

The big-band monopolist

Goldkette cornered so much of the Detroit area dance band business that he bought a ballroom, set up a booking office and sometimes had as many as six full-sized subsidiary orchestras playing simultaneously in and around Detroit. Goldkette himself would, on rare occasions, front one of his bands to please some high-society customer. In the fall of 1927 he sent a band under trumpeter Hank Biagini, with Spike Knoblauch playing lead alto and doubling on clarinet and baritone sax, to play at the Casa Loma luxury hotel in Toronto.

The Casa Loma is a vast and turreted pile of gray stone assembled during the period 1911-1914 as a private residence for Major General Sir Henry Mill Pellatt, a high-living soldier turned financier. Sir Henry spent $3,500,000 building and $1,500,000 furnishing his monument, which had its own private telephone system, an electric elevator, an indoor swimming pool, a 165-foot shooting gallery in the basement, one of the largest wine cellars on the North American continent, 15 bathrooms, 5,000 electric lights and a kitchen range which could roast an ox whole. The place employed forty servants whose wages set Sir Henry back some $22,000 a year. Sir Henry planned to spend the rest of his life in Casa

Loma and then will it to the city for a museum. Financial reverses forced him in 1923 to give up the plan and the castle. A corporation finally remodeled it into a hotel and hired the Orange Blossoms to help attract customers. The Blossoms played for eight months to appreciative listeners but never drew enough of them to make the place pay. Soon after the band returned to Detroit the hotel closed. It never reopened.

Part of Sir Henry's dream did come true. Toronto owns Casa Loma now, and the West Toronto Kiwanis Club runs it as a tourist attraction. Some 200,000 visitors a year now wander through the old place at $1.25 a head for adults, 35 cents for children, gaping at the stained glass windows of the conservatory and at the tunnel connecting the castle with the stables. Frequently a high school or other local group rents the ballroom for a dance, but nothing remains to show that Glen Gray's band got its start here.

Back in Detroit, Goldkette's enterprises were dissolving.

Casa Loma in Toronto, which gave Gray's band its name, began as a lavish private castle in 1914, was briefly a hotel.

The Casa Lomans line the Atlantic City boardwalk in 1931. When the sidemen autographed the picture in 1932, the line-up had changed; two new additions, Watts and Hutchenrider, put their names above the likenesses of their predecessors.

CASA LOMA ORCHESTRA

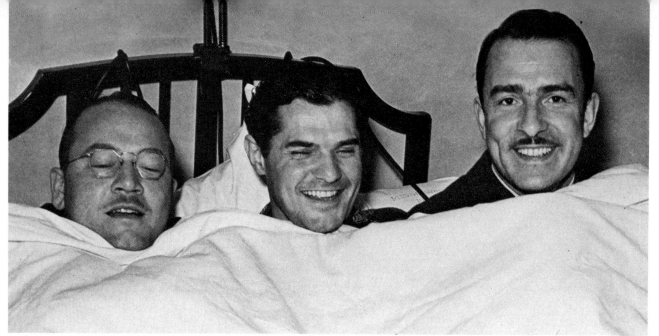

One-night stands (the band once played 101 straight weeks of them) could mean cramped quarters, but this three-in-a bed shot was strictly a press agent's idea. From the left are trombonist Pee Wee Hunt, singer Kenny Sargent and Gray.

He had spent $400,000 remodeling his Greystone Ballroom. His overhead, including a weekly $3,500 payroll, was high, and he had made some unprofitable outside investments. Competition was keener, public tastes in music were changing, and other bands steadily lured away top Goldkette sidemen. By the end of 1927 Goldkette had let go all but two of his bands, and they were not working steadily. By 1929 he was finished as a big band leader, though before he died in 1962 he achieved briefly his dream of organizing and leading a symphony orchestra.

The Goldkette unit led by Biagini was left jobless. "Glen had some money," Hunt recalls. "He was about the only one who did." At times like this, most bands dissolved. Most bands lacked a resourceful man like Spike. He was soon in touch with Francis ("Cork") O'Keefe who had been booking Goldkette bands in Detroit and was now in New York. With Cork's help, the band picked up a few bookings. Hunt recalls a gig in Pennsylvania, then one in Atlantic City under Roger Wolfe Kahn, the wealthy bandleader and jazz buff. After some one-nighters in New England, the band went into New York's Roseland Ballroom where the pay was only union scale but where bands the management liked got steady work. The management liked the eager young outfit which called itself (with Goldkette's blessing) Goldkette's Casa Loma Orchestra. The times were ripening for a big, jazz-oriented dance band, especially one which had the inspiration of a superb arranger like Gene Gifford and the stabilizing influence of a levelheaded Glen Gray.

Gifford was a shy, balding, bespectacled guitarist who admired Beethoven, Richard Strauss, Gustav Mahler and such distinguished jazz composer-arrangers as Don Redman. He was a banjo virtuoso. "He could play solos on it like a trumpet player," says Pee Wee Hunt. Gifford yearned to write for big ensembles and treasured every additional sideman, especially those who could double on several instruments, because they gave him more orchestral voices to write for.

The sidemen considered Gifford a genius. "He would lie in bed and write out a few bars of music," says Larry Wagner, "and I'd just marvel at the ideas the man was capable

of." Saxophonist Art Ralston remembers him "with a telephone cradled on his shoulder, listening to the radio, writing one arrangement with his right hand and another with his left, all at the same time." Trumpeter Grady Watts recalls that Gifford dashed off the melody for the band's famous theme, *Smoke Rings*, in the time it took Watts to leave their hotel room, descend to the lobby for a package of cigarettes, and return to see how Gifford was getting along.

A banjo to inspire the brass

Gifford gave the band its soul. Pee Wee Hunt remembers that his banjo "gave terrific inspiration to the brass section" and that "his ideas were for an ensemble jazz band, not a Dixieland band, but a big band." Few white arrangers had grasped this concept then, and the band's largely white audiences loved the new sound. The band's versatile alternation of fast and slow numbers, of jazz instrumentals and pop ballads, made it broadly appealing.

Gray gave the band continuity. Soon after reaching New York, the sidemen, acting in concert, fired Biagini as leader and formed a corporation with Glen Gray Knoblauch as president and Francis O'Keefe as business manager. Sidemen held all other corporate offices. The musicians shared the band's income equally, and as the band prospered their weekly shares increased. Because the corporation held salaries to a reasonable limit, it eventually had money left over after meeting all expenses. Any surplus was paid out in annual or semiannual dividends or invested. (The disappointing results of some of the investments were a sore point with a few Casa Lomans.) The stockholders met whenever necessary and wherever they happened to be to set rules like the fine ($50) for showing up for work drunk and to consider admissions of new members. Nobody got into the band unless he was someone the sidemen considered to be not only a first-rate instrumentalist but also personally congenial to the group. A writer of the period called Casa Loma "the band that's organized like a corporation and run like a college fraternity."

At one of their first meetings, the stockholders approved

Pee Wee Hunt's idea of hiring Mel Jenssen, a slim, handsome violinist, as a front man. Glen, everybody agreed, was a fine guy but he couldn't beat time. Jenssen could, and he fronted the band successfully for seven years.

It was a tough time to launch a new band. The stock market crashed on October 29, 1929, the day the Casa Lomans had made their first records, optimistically titled numbers like *Lucky Me, Lovable You* and *Happy Days Are Here Again*. The rather undistinguished Casa Loma versions of these pop tunes got lost amid the economic turmoil, but before long the Casa Loma band had scored a modest hit with a recording of Gene Gifford's arrangement of an old jazz favorite, *San Sue Strut*.

For the next couple of winters, the band lived in the Necho Allen Hotel in Pottsville, Pennsylvania, booked East Coast one-nighters wherever they could, and began accumulating fans one way or another. During various New England swings, Spike and two other sidemen, Pee Wee Hunt and trumpeter Joe Hostetter, all met and later married girls from Plymouth, Massachusetts. Spike's marriage to Marion Douglass lasted the rest of his life.

In December 1930 the band made more friends with three new recordings. *Casa Loma Stomp* was a catchy new riff tune. *Alexander's Ragtime Band* and *Put on Your Old Grey Bonnet* were old gray favorites which had been used as jazz vehicles before but never in a big band context. The solos, some of them improvised, were good for their time, and the bouncy, fast-paced arrangements made an instant hit with younger listeners. The pace was a lot faster, in fact, than arranger Gifford had intended. Glen, who set the tempos at rehearsals, still couldn't beat time. "They all became up-tempo flag-wavers as a result," says Hunt, "very flashy and sensational sounding."

Sensational sounds were in short supply in 1930. The crash of '29 had wiped out a lot of good jazz bands. Ben Pollack's band was still in business but had lost most of its stars and was making records which were far below its former best. Duke Ellington had yet to achieve an appreciable white audience. The great Fletcher Henderson made only

Gray is dressed to lead the band at a Texas barbecue during a 1939 engagement at the Majestic Theater in Fort Worth.

four records that whole year. The Casa Lomans had the biggest share of the market for big band jazz.

It was not much of a market at first. In 1930-31 the public and the record companies were leaning toward the soothing sounds of bands like Wayne King's and Guy Lombardo's. Glen and the band fought to keep some jazz in their repertory even when this meant playing for sparse crowds and cutting band salaries by half. The grind discouraged Jack Richmond, the band's big-voiced singer, who quit and was replaced by tall, handsome Kenny Sargent, a notable moaner of pop ballads. Pop ballads were about all the band recorded in 1931. Jack Kapp at Brunswick, the recording company with which Casa Loma had signed after the demise of OKeh, their original label, wanted nothing but nice sweet ballads like *Just a Blue-Eyed Blonde, Help Yourself to Happiness, Blue Kentucky Moon, If I Didn't Have You* and similar inanities. Kapp was right; the ballads sold well. But the boys wanted to play jazz, and on December 18, 1931, Kapp let them record a jazz standard, *Clarinet Marmalade*, and two Gifford originals, *Black Jazz* and *Maniac's Ball*, which introduced two new Casa Lomans, clarinetist Clarence Hutchenrider and trumpeter Grady Watts. Jazz fans liked the new numbers and the new stars, who were soon joined by a flashy young trumpeter-trombonist-arranger, Sonny Dunham. Gifford happily began writing for three trombones, then a new device. He also whipped out *Smoke Rings* in which he blended three clarinets with Billy Rauch's muted trombone to give Casa Loma the most distinctive theme song of any band in the business.

No Casa Loman grew rich in 1932, but the band never

Gray and Eleanor Roosevelt meet at a 1938 Presidential birthday ball. The band was heard over a 500-station hookup.

lacked work. It once played a consecutive string of one hundred and one weeks of one-nighters, a figure probably unequaled by any band of the period. That fall things began picking up. O'Keefe booked the band into a series of Midwest engagements, including a stretch at the Bellerive Hotel in Kansas City. "The guy who had the place wanted the band," O'Keefe recalls, "but he was scared of it because of all the jazz. All he had had in there before were guys like Wayne King." To pacify him, O'Keefe imported Johnny ("Scat") Davis as front man, but the band got rid of Davis in short order by systematic sabotage. "We just didn't want anyone else up there in front of the band after all the rough times we had come through," Gifford recalled shortly before his death in 1970. After hours, the Casa Lomans had a ball sitting in on sessions in the jumping joints of Kansas City, then the world's hottest jazz spot.

The band began getting more college and prep-school prom dates. In May 1933 it played at the Lawrenceville School in New Jersey. Two of William Randolph Hearst's sons reportedly flew in for the event in a plane borrowed from their father, and CBS made it the occasion for the network's first broadcast of a school or college dance. Offers poured in, and the band's price jumped from around $200 an evening to as much as $1,200. The manager of Glen Island Casino caught the band at a Yale prom and signed it up for the whole summer. "We knew we had it made then," says Grady Watts.

The businessman's bounce

Back at the Brunswick studios Jack Kapp was hollering for more ballads. Gene Gifford, to the surprise of the rest of the band, amicably turned out a flock of romantic arrangements, which the band played in a style that would have melted a statue. In those days, if you danced to the music of Guy Lombardo or Rudy Vallee, you had to keep moving to what musicians called the businessman's bounce, a medium fox-trot tempo. Casa Loma played many of the same tunes but much slower than anybody else. You didn't have to concentrate on your dancing. You could just stand there swaying gracefully, holding your girl and letting the rich Casa Loma ensemble of saxes and brass soak through you while Kenny Sargent, with a voice like molasses, sang *Under a Blanket of Blue* or *For You*.

For You was such a hit that Kenny had to sing it just about every night of his professional career, but success never brought him self-confidence. "Why do you keep me singing?" he used to ask Glen.

By 1933 the band had long since dropped Goldkette from its title and was recording under the name of Glen Gray and His Orchestra or Glen Gray and the Casa Loma Orchestra. People were beginning to ask Cork O'Keefe, "Is there a Mr. Casa Loma?" Cork told Spike, "We have to have more of an identification. Get your name changed legally to Glen Gray." Spike did, though he had a hard time explaining to Uncle Ed back in Metamora, Illinois, why "Gray" would look better on a marquee than "Knoblauch." Then people wondered why "Glen Gray" was sitting in the sax section instead of waving a baton. "I'm not paying thousands of dollars for Glen Gray and his Casa Loma Orchestra if he's not out there in front of the band where people can see him," fumed a Detroit theater manager. "Get him in front of the band!" In

1937 Mel Jenssen went back to Ohio to open a night club, and Glen fronted the band. "He was awful," says Grady Watts. "It got so we wouldn't pay any attention to him." As Art Ralston remembers it, "We would see that downbeat come down three seconds late, so we stopped following his lead, and eventually he began following us." The tall, well-built, handsome Gray, with his movie-star mustache and his brilliant smile, at least met all the requirements of the public's image of a bandleader.

The sidemen appreciated more Gray's other contributions to the band. Nobody else, they felt, could have held the band together through the hard days, kept it steadfastly on its chosen course, and brought it triumphantly into lush dates at the best hotels and three straight years on the Camel Caravan.

Few bandleaders got so much good music out of their men with so little ill-feeling as the easygoing Gray. "Spike never raised his voice," says guitarist Herb Ellis. "You'd just see his mustache start to twitch when he got mad, which wasn't very often."

Hardly anybody else could have handled so successfully an eccentric like the unworldly Gene Gifford, who used to stuff his hotel closets with dirty laundry until they could hold no more, then move to another hotel and go out and buy more shirts and socks. Gifford, who could repair any musical instrument, was also a car nut. His automobiles were always rapidly repossessed because he could never keep up the payments. Gifford, untroubled, would simply put down a first payment on another. He took apart a fire-engine-red Chrysler and reassembled it in such a way that he achieved, in Art Ralston's firm opinion, the world's first automatic gearshift.

Gray was sensitive, too, about pulling his weight in the sax section. Ralston tactfully talked him into switching from alto sax, on which Art says he had a "milky" sound, to tenor. The band saw to it that the arrangers wrote some nice tenor parts for Glen. The move strengthened a band which by the mid-'30s had become one of the smoothest, most profitable musical machines in the business. The sidemen reflected the band's success. "I remember going to Brisk's on 49th Street," says Ralston, "and getting four complete sets of uniforms at $350 apiece, and that's in 1933! We always wore full dress complete with tails while most other bands wore tuxedos. We wore platinum cuff links and shirt studs and displayed a pocket watch which cost around a thousand dollars."

Gray's success had shown the way. By the end of 1936 Benny Goodman was King of Swing and had replaced Casa Loma on the Camel Caravan. Great new swing bands emerged on every hand. Gray remained serene. "There's always room for one more at the top," he said to Ralston after Goodman's rush to fame. "Why should I worry about him? We're a sweet band. So he has all the kids. We had them too and they were great, but the ones we had are grown up now and earning good money. We have a different audience."

The Casa Loma audience was astonishingly faithful. The band topped the 1939 *Metronome* poll in the "Sweet" category. "This was the greatest band in the country for making friends," says Ralston. "Whenever we'd go into a town, the guys would call up the people they had met the first time they were there, and those people never forgot it. In any hotel we were staying or playing we got to know everyone from the managing director right down to the waiters, chambermaids, busboys and boiler-room attendants. The people we knew would flock to wherever we were playing. During the eight years I was with the band, I never remember a dance we played that wasn't absolutely packed, and most of them they had to turn people away from the door. This is all through the time when Goodman and the others were riding high, too."

Larry Clinton remembered one road trip with the band: "Every town we went into en route none of the guys ever had to eat in restaurants, and often they slept in private homes. It was fantastic."

The Casa Loma Orchestra never lost its fans, just the means of reaching them. By 1941 wartime conditions and the number of bands available sharply reduced long-term bookings. The Casa Loma Orchestra could always get a gig

but it meant a lot of one-nighters, and the veterans began dropping out to take secure studio jobs and to be with their families. The corporation was dissolved in 1942, but the band played on. The sound wasn't quite the same but Glen Gray could still attract talented musicians like trumpeters Red Nichols and Bobby Hackett, drummer Cliff Leeman, Herb Ellis the guitarist and arranger Ray Conniff. Fatigue and diabetes forced Glen to give up the band at the end of 1947. In 1950, after an eight-month comeback attempt, he finally conceded that the big band days were over.

Gray died in 1963. His monuments are many. Record sales which were impressive even in years of depression. The warm regard of practically every sideman who ever played for him. And the assurance that Glen Gray and the Casa Loma Orchestra not only made some nice music but gave the Swing Era a timely push.   —FRANK DRIGGS

Dapper as ever, even for a recording session, Gray (*left*) confers with trombonist Ray Benson (*center*) and alto saxophon-

ist Skeets Herfurt in 1956 when Gray was making a series of Casa Loma and other re-creations for Capitol Records.

The Men Who Made the Music:
Raymond Scott

The Raymond Scott Quintet contributed to the Swing Era a unique blend of rhythms, harmonies and sound effects conceived by a man who was as much engineer as musician and who never put his music on paper. He led five excellent musicians who resentfully admired their leader and generally disliked their work.

The leader, Raymond Scott, achieved his remarkable results by insisting on perfection. "All he ever had was machines," says Scott's former drummer, Johnny Williams, "only we had names."

Scott composed, not on paper, but on his Quintet. He would play a phrase on the piano and say, "Try that, Dave." After listening to saxophonist Dave Harris play the phrase, Scott would either tell him to remember it or would try for an idea he might like better. Then he would go on to another instrument. "It was a very extravagant way to compose," says trumpeter Dave Wade. Scott also recorded rehearsals of the Quintet, played the recordings at night and combined phrases he liked into new recordings. Then the Quintet, which never used written music, would listen to and memorize these montages.

"He didn't write anything, but he edited everything," says Williams. "We would work these things up and we would never change them, ever. We had to do them note for note. It was highly unsatisfactory and it sold like hell."

Raymond Scott, originally Harry Warnow, was born in Brooklyn on September 10, 1909, son of Joseph Warnow, a diamond merchant who was also an amateur violinist, and his wife Sarah. The Warnows had arrived from their native Russia two years before with their five-year-old son Mark. Both boys were musically inclined. A family legend says that Harry at the age of two accompanied his father on the piano. "As a child, I had no real musical training," says Scott, "just piano lessons of the fifty-cent variety." He also developed a flair for the dramatic, for descriptive music and for electrical engineering.

At twelve he hung Japanese lanterns all over the family dining room to create mood lighting. At fifteen, when he was working as a pianist in upstate New York summer resorts, he was thinking in terms of musical portraits. "I'd see a cow and I'd think, 'How can I portray that cow in music?'" He spent hours in the phonograph shop his father had opened when Harry was six "playing recordings for the cus-

tomers and learning electronics by fooling around with the stock." He talked Mark into turning their bedroom into an audio laboratory.

Mark talked Harry out of going to Brooklyn Polytech and becoming an engineer. Mark was by then a prospering violinist. "He said I was too talented musically to go into engineering," says Scott. "He bought me a Steinway and paid my tuition to the Institute of Musical Art." When Harry graduated in 1931 from what later became the Juilliard School, Mark talked him into becoming staff pianist for the CBS radio orchestra.

As conductor of the CBS house band, Mark promoted the music of Harry Warnow and other American composers, but the brothers felt "it was a bit sticky for him to be playing my music" so Harry became "Raymond Scott," a name they picked out of the Manhattan telephone directory because "it was a nice sounding name, it had good rhythm to it."

Scott spent five fairly tranquil years as a staff pianist. He married Pearl Stevens, a New York girl of Russian parentage, and began working fulltime on his own compositions.

"He was very quiet," says Louis Shoobe, then the bass player in the Warnow band and now in charge of hiring and assigning all musicians for CBS in New York. "He'd eat, sleep and drink the piano, always working out thoughts of what he could do musically." By 1936, however, the quiet pianist was getting restless. He complained repeatedly to CBS producer Herb Rosenthal that the network house band played the same music all the time. "So finally Rosenthal said, 'Okay, wise guy, we'll give you some of the fellows from the band and let's see what you can do.'"

Scott picked bassist Shoobe, tenor saxophonist Harris, clarinetist Pete Pumiglio, drummer Williams and trumpeter Bunny Berigan, who soon quit. "It took up too much of his time," says Shoobe. Dave Wade replaced Berigan in what became the six-man Raymond Scott Quintet. Scott says he thought "quintet" sounded nicer than "sextet." Some of the sidemen felt, like Berigan, that Scott was taking up too much of their time with his interminable rehearsals, but they stuck with him, fascinated, perhaps, by the unusual sound he was gradually achieving.

Al Brackman was then an associate producer for the Master recording company run by Irving Mills, Duke Ellington's shrewd and perceptive manager. "Someone told me about this wild guy—an engineer-pianist-composer-arranger—who had been rehearsing one song for eight months," Brackman recalls. "I went over to CBS to listen to them—they were rehearsing *The Toy Trumpet* for Mark Warnow's Christmas show—and they absolutely knocked me out."

The Toy Trumpet also knocked out just about everybody who heard the Quintet in its first public performance on that Saturday Night Swing Session on December 26, 1936. The gay little tune with its rhythmic bounce provided the ideal setting for the tiny, tinny, yet musically perfect trumpet sound. The music had the slight satiric edge which set Scott's creations apart from all other Swing Era novelty numbers. Brackman could see that Scott's tricky, easy-to-listen-to numbers would have an instant wide appeal. He urged Scott to record for the Mills label.

A mike in the men's room

"My group won't be ready for a couple of years," said Scott. "I've written the music, but it's taken us all this time just to get one song right." But Mills persuaded Scott that now was the time to make it big. Scott astounded the recording engineers when, early in 1937, he recorded a dozen or so sides for Mills. "Our studio at 1776 Broadway was basically just an office with a seven- or eight-foot ceiling," says Brackman. "There was a long hall leading to it from the elevators and, opposite the office door, a men's room lined with tiles. Scott insisted on recording at night so he could put one mike in the hall and another in the men's room. With that and the other mikes in the office he achieved what they call 'echo' and gave the recordings a big auditorium sound."

The Depression was still a fact of American life in the winter of 1936-37 and record sales were slow, but the first Scott record Mills released, *Twilight in Turkey* backed by *Minuet in Jazz*, sold out within a week. "It had nothing to compete with it," says Brackman. "If you liked Scott, you had to buy Scott."

More records followed rapidly. By no coincidence, their titles were as catchy as the tunes. It was all one process with Scott who would dream up an unlikely situation, compress it into a title and then describe it in numbers like *War Dance for Wooden Indians* or *Dinner Music for a Pack of Hungry Cannibals*. The music had more than just gimmicks like the oriental theme, minor-key slides and tiny cymbals in *Twilight in Turkey*, the hiss of machinery and beat of pistons in *Powerhouse* and the happy slap and shuffle of flat feet in *Huckleberry Duck*. It had wit and sparkle as well as a beat as steady as a metronome, though sometimes so fast that you wondered how anyone could hit all the notes.

"There was a unity of spirit," says Scott, recalling the perfection of those early Quintet recordings. "Everybody was brilliant, everyone loved what I was doing and I loved what they were doing. There's a tremendous difference in per-

Racketing across New York's Lake George in a rented outboard, Raymond Scott looks relaxed during a 1935 vacation.

Scott called his six-man group a "quintet," a word he liked better than "sextet." In 1938, when they were all with CBS, the group included (*from left*) Dave Harris, Louis Shoobe, Peewee Erwin, Johnny Williams, Scott and Pete Pumiglio.

formance if you skip the eyes." Lots of bands, of course, "skipped the eyes" when they made "head" arrangements without initially putting anything on paper. Few bands ever had such a large and precisely memorized unwritten library as the Quintet's.

"If I played something on the piano," says Scott, "and they picked it up on their instruments, it took on a tremendous strength of feeling. They would hear the spirit and play back the spirit."

"Scott's music was difficult," says Shoobe. "A lot of his ideas were pianistic and hard to translate to another instrument. If you didn't like it, you couldn't do it. But once you got started you could get the idea. You worked and you got it. I don't think you could do it under another conductor. After I left Scott, I worked under another conductor who tried some of that music, and I couldn't even do my own part."

"We really didn't want to do any of it," Johnny Williams demurs. "So there we were, doing what he called descriptive jazz and which we thought was descriptive all right but not jazz, because jazz is right now, not memorized note for note. And after all this compulsive rehearsal, suddenly it all caught on and we were making more money than anybody else in town, all thanks to him. We were doing records, public appearances, making movies, everything."

"Just plain luck," says Scott of the group's popularity. "The true way to be an artist is to write what you feel and hope you're lucky enough so that other people like it, too."

Plenty of people liked it. He was, as jazz critic Frederic Ramsey Jr. explains, spreading a jazz-like sound among peo-

ple unaccustomed to jazz. Hollywood liked it. Seven months after their first radio broadcast, the Quintet was under contract to 20th Century-Fox. Scott spent a year composing for the movies on his six-voiced instrument. Twentieth Century used three of his already recorded tunes in three movies. After a year, Scott returned to New York saying he had found the movie makers undiscriminating. "They think everything is wonderful." CBS thought he was pretty wonderful, too, and put at his disposal any studios, recording equipment, engineers, arrangers or musicians he wanted. Presumably, CBS recognized Scott as a hot property and a man from whom something might be learned. "Scott was in the vanguard of achieving new electronic balances," says Ramsey. "He foreshadows all that was to come years later."

"The music was harmonically innovative," says Dave Harris. "When I listened to the Tijuana Brass a few years ago I heard things we'd done thirty years before."

CBS held onto its visionary star for two years. Then Scott, seeking new challenges, organized his own band, using some of his former Quintet musicians, and hit the road. He worked hard to bring the whole band up to Quintet standards. "The Quintet had super-super musicians. It was a terribly lucky accident. I like both the Quintet and the orchestra, but they were different mediums. In both it was the creative process, the joy of practicing."

Not everybody enjoyed practicing as much as Scott. "When we were on the road," says Shoobe, "we'd ask him to go to the movies, but he'd say no. We'd leave him playing the piano and when we came back he'd be playing the piano. Time meant nothing to him."

Scott tried to get as much fun as possible out of his band performances. He conned audiences with silent finales, the band getting softer and softer toward the end of a piece while making larger and larger motions. Then, while his listeners strained to catch every nuance, "we'd fake the sound for two or three minutes, still using the large-scale motions." Scott also used to march the band off the stage and out into the audience and then lead a number with his men scattered around the auditorium. "The audience loved it," he says with childlike wonder. "I've never heard applause like that in my life. I was so excited about that."

Scott's band tours were financially successful, though some critics complained that the music was too choppy for dancing, but he gave up the road in 1942 and returned to CBS. "I didn't like public appearances," he says. "I was meant to be an engineer."

He became a CBS music director and organized a big studio band. It was the first such group to include black artists, hired at the suggestion of John Hammond who had long been working to erase music's color line, and included men like trumpeter Charlie Shavers, trombonist Benny Morton, bassist Israel Crosby, drummer Specs Powell and saxophonist Ben Webster.

Scott also organized a new Quintet of jazz stars such as trumpeter Emmett Berry, saxophonist Jerry Jerome, pianist Mel Powell and drummer Cozy Cole. Scott and these sidemen never seemed to find the same wavelength. "We came up against ideas that just didn't meet ours," says Berry who never reconciled his own warm approach to jazz with Scott's demands for perfection.

Scott continued happily and relentlessly drilling his big studio band and broadcasting from a tiny studio to which his electronic magic lent the sound of a large auditorium. "That 1944 band was remarkable," he says. "We had the best musicians, and we rehearsed four and a half hours every day for a half-hour show."

"It was a pretty band," recalls Shavers. "It wasn't a swing band and it wasn't a jazz band, it was a good band with a good bunch of guys. Scott was a little eccentric. He'd make a guy stand up and play third alto, all by himself, all the way through. And then he'd say, 'Why don't you go take some lessons?' He got on my nerves a little. We'd rehearse and rehearse and *rehearse*. We didn't need that much rehearsal. I think he just liked to hear the band.

"He finally blew me out. We were rehearsing a piece and my part lay up around high D. We must have rehearsed that thing thirty times. We got on the air and I was blowed out. It was my solo and I couldn't hit it. So I let sixteen bars go by, then I picked up the horn and made the ending." Never again, Shavers promised himself. "Whenever he'd start to rehearse me too much, I'd just say, 'Do you want it now or do you want it on the air?' Or sometimes I'd just go down to the men's room and stay downstairs until three minutes before air time."

One of the few shows to survive the leap from radio to video was Your Hit Parade. Scott helped, having taken over the band when his brother Mark died in 1949. Here, in shirt sleeves *(center, rear)*, he rehearses a TV production number.

Pianist Johnny Guarnieri also found Scott unnerving. "He would tell you how lousy you were and then take you to lunch." In the studio, Guarnieri missed the interchange of feeling between artist and audience but felt that this never bothered Scott. "Scott was clinical; his life was stopwatches."

Scott feels that the artist, to succeed, must "temporarily defeat human nature . . . become temporarily superhuman."

Even former Scott sidemen who do not share this rather remote and chilling view of success admit some debts to Scott. "I developed a terrible desire to become perfect myself," says Guarnieri. And Williams admits, "All that discipline helped. It had to. I developed a technique way beyond what I'd had."

Hobby: blind driving

Scott also developed a technique for giving colorful interviews. "I like to improvise in music and speech," he says. "I just enjoyed saying colorful things when people came to interview me. I couldn't comprehend that people were really interested in the plainer things, like what I ate for breakfast, so I would make it entertaining. When they asked me what my hobbies were I said I liked blind driving—like blind flying, only on the road."

Soon stories abounded that Scott drove with his eyes shut, that he gave autographs in invisible ink and that he had tried to park his car in his living room. "A Buick makes a handsome piece of furniture," he had told one reporter.

"After a while it got so nutty and wild that it backfired," Scott says. "When my name came up for a job, people would think twice. I gave it up."

Having achieved the ideal studio band in 1944, Scott naturally became restless again. In 1945 he again left CBS, organized yet another big band and returned to the road. Scott soon gave up the tour, however, to write the score for a Broadway show, *Lute Song*. Scott knew nothing about writing a show and, as usual, put nothing on paper, dictating everything to musical secretaries. Oddly enough, a score emerged and the musical, starring Mary Martin and Yul Brynner, was produced to mild critical acclaim. One of the pretty songs from Scott's score, *Mountain High, Valley Low*, is still selling as sheet music and has been variously recorded, most recently by Morgana King.

After *Lute Song*, Scott managed in various ways to keep busy. He organized a new dance band and toured briefly with it. Then he organized another Quintet, the personnel of which changed constantly, with which he toured and did a two-year stint on the Herb Shriner Show. He started his own recording company, reactivating the defunct Master label, and sold by direct mail renditions by his shifting ensemble of such new Scott inspirations as *Snakewoman*, *Bird Walk in the Bronx* and *Dedicatory Piece to the Crew and Passengers of the First Experimental Rocket Ship to the Moon*. This last was written in 1947, exactly twenty-one years before the first manned lunar orbit. The Apollo 8 astronauts had a happier return than the rocketmen Scott imagined. "When they get back," he said, explaining the eerie ending of his piece, "there's been an atom war and nobody's around."

In October 1949 Scott's brother Mark died and NBC asked Scott to take over the Hit Parade show on which Mark had led the band for twelve years. (The Hit Parade began life with NBC, shifted to CBS from 1936 to 1947, returned to NBC in 1947 and died there in 1959.) For the next eight years Scott led the Hit Parade, successfully supervising its transition from radio to TV.

The energies not absorbed by conducting the hits of the week Scott turned into other channels. For Lucky Strike, the Hit Parade's sponsor, he wrote in 1950 a jingle, as singing commercials were then called, entitled *Be Happy, Go Lucky*. It was a hit, and Scott began turning out similar persuasive melodies for Barbasol, General Motors, Nescafé and Anacin.

Scott and his wife Pearl were divorced in 1950. Two years later he married Dorothy Collins, a pretty young Hit Parade vocalist who had sung with his late '40s band and Quintet. She and Scott were separated in 1965.

During the Hit Parade years Scott also was busily building electronic devices in his Long Island home. The first was Karloff, a $100,000 gadget on which he and a fulltime technician started work in 1948. Karloff began by making a sound used to help sell a sore-chest remedy, and the versatile machine went on to imitate such saleable sounds as kitchen clatter, the sizzle of frying steak and jungle drums.

Karloff was not particularly musical, but the Clavivox, which Scott perfected in 1957, was. It is the first keyboard instrument which can slide from one note to another, like a voice or a wind instrument, without a break. Its variety of voices are reminiscent of human, brass and woodwind sounds. Bruce Haack, a composer and inventor, has featured the Clavivox on an album of electronic music, and Scott says he has had an order for five Clavivoxes from somebody in Tunis.

It was also in 1957 that the Hit Parade's sponsor decided to give the show a new look and fired Scott and his wife, among others. Scott was philosophical. "It's a wonder that the cast has been kept intact so long," he said. "On radio, it used to change every thirteen weeks or so." Soon after, he gave up his Jingle Workshop, explaining that it was no fun now that "everyone has access to electronic equipment." Scott likes to be out ahead of the field. In 1958 he switched most of his attention to creating a revolutionary electronic instrument. By 1970 he had it ready for production.

A cockpit of dreams

The Electronium, as Scott envisions it, will be a semicircular affair, with panels of switches and dials, rather like a cross between an organ and a spaceship simulator. "I want the Electronium to be a beautiful instrument," he says, "to have a sort of special feeling, like a Steinway. Not to look like a Steinway, of course, but to have that sense of elegance and beauty. And I want it to have the feeling of driving, a steering machine, a cockpit of dreams."

The home of the Electronium is Raymond Scott Enterprises, located in a long, one-story cement block building in an industrial park in Farmingdale, Long Island. At the reception desk is Scott's pert, redheaded third wife Mitzi, a former dancer and pianist. In the next room, girls at long tables thread circuit boards with colored wires, humming to Muzak as they work. A second room is a heavy-duty machine shop. In the third room sits the Electronium. Small colored lights blink silently. Scott says the machine is thinking. If you can believe that, you can believe Scott's assertion that, together with a human operator, the machine composes music which can then be recorded on tape.

"It's like inventing the typewriter," says Scott, "only the typewriter furnishes the plot and reads the result in its own voice. You specify the form and structure, but the details are the machine's. If you like what the machine does but want a different key or tempo, you push the appropriate button. For the talented and trained person wielding its switches, the Electronium will give a most comprehensive performance."

Scott already has an order for a $100,000 version of the machine from a buyer who wishes to remain anonymous.

("Which is a shame," says Scott. "I was hoping to get some publicity from it.") Eventually he hopes to market $1,200 versions for private enjoyment or public performance. He feels it will be excellent for TV and film scoring. "It's very moody and goes with video." He hopes to build still other instruments "that will represent incredible breakthroughs."

Meanwhile, he and the Electronium (Scott always gives the machine equal billing) have composed numerous pieces including a "classical" *Iceberg Theme, The Wild Piece* ("my super-Stravinsky") and *Take Me to Your Violin Teacher.* This last one is about the arrival on Earth of beings from another world where violin-playing is the supreme art. It shows, if anything, that the Electronium picks up styles adroitly. The piece sounds a lot like the work of the Raymond Scott Quintet.   —MICHÈLE WOOD

An electronics music man almost before there was any such thing, Raymond Scott spends most of his time creating ingenious devices in his Long Island workshop. His Clavivox

(foreground) can make woodwind, brass or human-sounding tones. The Electronium, parts of which surround the inventor, is a machine which Scott says composes music.

The Music in This Volume

It was the bright morning of swing—those years of 1937 and 1938. The music had both discipline and a rare freshness. The musicians had new assurance and a little more money. And the listeners, cheering and screaming, had a growing host of idols for their pantheon—Benny and Tommy, Artie and Bunny, the Count and the Duke, Lunceford and Casa Loma and a nut named Scott (at least his music sounded nutty). The youngsters kept swinging from early morning, when they stormed into the Paramount or the Strand to dance and faint in the aisles, until late night when they stayed up for the coast-to-coast broadcasts from California. Benny Goodman had ignited the Swing Era with his historic success at the Palomar in Los Angeles. Now he was spreading the fire at another level with swing's first Carnegie Hall concert.

Not everybody applauded. Traditional musicians snorted that swing couldn't last, grown-ups grumped at the goings-on, and a psychiatrist bemoaned the "dangerously hypnotic influence of swing, cunningly devised to a faster tempo than seventy-two bars to the minute—faster than the human pulse." This got him and his cantankerous cohorts nowhere. In Metronome's 1937 poll of most popular bands, five of the top six played swing, and the 1938 winner in Down Beat's sweet category was the Casa Loma, which played as much swing as sweet. "Must be pretty much of a nasty sock in the face," declared Metronome, "for all those would-be smart guys who, because they can't play it or else don't know what it's all about, insist that swing is just a fad on its way out."

SIDE ONE

Band 1 DON'T BE THAT WAY
Benny Goodman version

Year in and year out, there were two numbers that Benny Goodman always had to play for his audiences: *Stompin' at the Savoy* (which is re-created in the 1936-37 album of THE SWING ERA) and *Don't Be That Way*. Both were written and arranged by Edgar Sampson for Chick Webb's band, but both were far more popular in Goodman's version than in Webb's. Each of them shows off Sampson's skill at weaving a simple phrase through many repetitions without dulling it. In *Don't Be That Way* the theme is stated first by the unison saxes with brasses dropping syncopated accents. When the clarinet takes a felicitous solo, the saxes provide a contrasting figure. The clarinet shares choruses with a bristly trumpet and a relaxed trombone. And the piece ends with the saxes repeating the theme over and over in diminishing volume until a drum break brings on the brilliant closing.

A simple song like this requires almost faultless treatment. "Sampson had a certain idea in mind when he wrote it that way," Goodman says in his autobiography, *The Kingdom of Swing*, "and it was up to us to play the way he wanted it. . . . When we first rehearsed it, some of the fellows were playing a triplet kind of uneven, with more time on one note than another, instead of making them all even. Well, we went over that and rehearsed it . . . till everybody was playing it just the same way. That was one of the reasons that we got such a terrific rock on that arrangement and why it turned out to be one of the biggest things we ever had." And that unrelenting demand for perfection was one reason why some musicians couldn't put up with Goodman as a leader—and why those who could produced such superb swing.

Band 2 SLEEPY TIME GAL
Glen Gray version

Great musical art this isn't. Swing it barely is. But memories? Ah, memories . . .

The floor is a dark pool of shadows and those familiar trumpet and clarinet phrases bring you out to dance. You glide slowly, cheek coming closer to cheek, as the trombones melt through their chorus. The mellow clarinet begins, and you open your eyes to watch the dabs of colored lights, reflected from the revolving glass globe overhead, play across the floor and your partner's face—gold followed by blue followed by pink followed by violet followed by gold. The beat softens. You stop dancing and just sway as the trombone starts on the part you love best: up on the bandstand a serious little man named Billy Rauch is standing and playing as if his heart were in his horn. The cymbal shakes you out of your reverie and starts you dancing again. The beat keeps you moving until the trumpets and clarinet that brought you on the floor now send you off to walk dreamily, fingers entwined, back to your table to finish your Scotch and ginger ale.

Sleepy Time Gal! Eheu, fugaces—and you can say that again.

Band 3 ANNIE LAURIE
Jimmie Lunceford version

Yes, there really was an Annie Laurie. She lived in the early 1700s in a castle on Maxwelton's braes and, according to an old *Ballad Book*, was "much celebrated for her beauty & made a conquest of Mr. Douglas of Fingland who composed verses under an unlucky star, for the lady married Mr. Fergusson of Cragdarroch."

That is only the bare bones of the story. Annie was not only beautiful but willful, and Willie Douglas was not just a poet but a local rake. Annie was enraptured by the love lyric he wrote to her but her parents would have none of Willie. They locked their daughter in her stone-walled bedroom until she agreed to marry Alexander Fergusson, a respectable neighboring laird. Neither Annie nor Willie stayed lovelorn for very long. She became a contented wife and he soon married another.

Long after both had died, Willie's poem was discovered by Lady John Scott, a formidable Scottish noblewoman who dabbled in song. In the 1830s she wrote a melody for the verse while at the same time severely editing the lyrics. Willie's own words were on the lusty side. His second stanza, for example, went: "She's backit like the peacock She's briestit like the swan; She's jimp about the middle, Her waist ye weel micht span . . . And she has a rolling eye. . . ." Lady Scott's genteel version goes: "Her brow is like the snowdrift, Her neck is like the swan, Her face it is the fairest, That e'er the sun shone on . . . And dark blue is her e'e. . . ."

Lunceford's *Annie Laurie*, as arranged by Sy Oliver, is much closer in feeling to Willie Douglas' earthy original than Lady Scott's bowdlerized version. It explodes out of the last few bars of the old song into a chorus and on into a driving succession of brass ensembles, off-beat saxophone accents, marching trombones, a belligerent tenor sax, a raw-voiced trombone and a screaming trumpet. All in all, Annie comes on more like a belting blues shouter than a bonnie Highland lassie.

Band 4 SUMMERTIME
Bob Crosby version

In 1935 George Gershwin summoned friends to his apartment to let them hear the score for his most ambitious project, *Porgy and Bess*. Sitting down at the piano, he sang *Summertime* in his croaky voice. The listeners were delighted with it until he told them that it was to be the opera's opening number. A simple song like that, they argued, was no way to start an opera. Something big was needed—a chorus or a production number. "This will work out just fine, wait and see," said Gershwin, and he was right, as usual.

The Crosby band gave the lullaby its most tender treatment. The chime-like piano chords of the introduction recur throughout, reinforcing the prevailing minor-mode feeling. The melody is blown by a combination of clarinets and saxophones similar to the voicing soon to be made famous by Glenn Miller. The tenor sax plays a plaintive solo, originally done by Eddie

Miller, whose tone was so pure that critics compared it to the purest commodity around, Ivory Soap.

Summertime became the Crosby theme song and, considering that what the men did best were fast two-beat Dixie numbers, it seems odd that they should have wanted to be identified by so sleepy a song. As Gil Rodin, who managed the band, explains it: "We'd been playing the *Porgy and Bess* score, and *Summertime* sounded so beautiful we all thought wouldn't it make a fantastic theme. We got Gershwin to come over and hear us. He was very impressed and gave us permission to use *Summertime* as a theme. We loved that tune."

Band 5 EVERY TUB
Count Basie version

This is one of those up-tempo head arrangements that the Basie band was doing so superbly during its first years in New York. It was built, as most of them were, on a riff the band had latched onto—this time a phrase reminiscent of *Christopher Columbus*, the famous Fletcher Henderson number re-created in the 1936-37 album of THE SWING ERA. Eddie Durham, who played trombone and solo guitar in the band, also took on the job of making arrangements out of the band's improvisations. "Basie and Eddie," says Dicky Wells, the trombonist, "would lock up in a room with a jug, and Basie would play the ideas and Eddie would voice them." It wasn't all that simple, according to Durham. "That guy Basie," he says, "was just full of ideas, but you could never hold him still for more than eight bars."

The song's title comes from a black ghetto adage, "Every tub sits on its own bottom," meaning that every man has to stand on his own. The band took the maxim to heart. "Each soloist," explains Durham, "ad-libs with his own ideas. It's every man for himself." In the opening tenor sax solo (played originally by Lester Young), the notes come out hard and polished. A piano (originally Basie) plays confidently and the trumpet stutters through a chorus. The sections toss the main riff back and forth, letting up for some short solos (the rapid tenor sax was originally Herschel Evans), and then settling into a repetition of the riff.

But it is less the soloists who make this piece than the band, which seems to be having such an exuberant time with it. "I never in my life had the feeling of music or any kind of feeling like I got when I joined Basie," says Earle Warren, who led the saxophone section for many years. "I could hardly wait to get to the ballroom to tune up. You'd run in and say hello and listen to the stories the guys tell, and you laughed and got a happy feeling and you spent such a beautiful evening."

SIDE TWO
Band 1 BLUE AND SENTIMENTAL
Count Basie version

Several aspects of *Blue and Sentimental* set it apart from other Basie songs. One is its form: it is, among all the Count's *jives*, *jumps* and *bounces*, his only romantic ballad. Another rarity is the famous clarinet soloist, Lester Young—who was famous, however, for playing the tenor sax, not the clarinet. But what gives *Blue and Sentimental* a special place in swing are the rhapsodic tenor saxophone solos played originally by Herschel Evans, who crowded a whole lifetime of fine music into his two and a half years with Basie.

The Evans saxophone, as re-created by Plas Johnson in this recording, comes on right after the introduction—soft and warm, dark but not somber, with a vibrato that is more felt than heard. After a delicately embroidered piano passage and a muted trombone, the clarinet takes its solo. It is forceful and skillful but hardly suggests Young's radically inventive saxophone. The

Evans sax thrusts its way back into the ensemble and plays almost alone in a final heartfelt passage.

Evans, a Texan, was brought up to Kansas City by his cousin, Eddie Durham, who himself was starting his distinguished career as trombonist, guitarist and arranger. "He was playing the alto," says Durham, "but his tone was so bad we had to put him on tenor. Herschel wasn't like most of those tenor sax men—they clown around and they overtalk. He was a quiet man." Evans joined Basie in Kansas City in 1936 and almost immediately, he and Lester Young launched into their legendary tenor sax rivalry. Evans' style—emotional and melting in the slow numbers, impetuous in the fast ones (as in *Every Tub* on Side 1 of this album)—contrasted with Young's cooler, controlled approach. Basie made the most of his two battling tenors. "When Young started a solo," remembers trombonist Dicky Wells, "part of the crowd would stand up and cheer him. When Evans took his, the rest of the crowd would stand up and cheer him." The musical feud never developed into personal bitterness. "Even when Hersh and Les weren't talking to each other," explained Wells, "they were still friends." The rivalry was sadly short-lived. In 1939 Evans died of heart failure. No one mourned him more than Young. "I was the last to see him before he died," he said. "I even paid his doctor's bills. He was a nice person. He loved his instrument and I loved mine."

Band 2 WHAT IS THIS THING CALLED LOVE?
Artie Shaw version

Artie Shaw had begun to capitalize on his fondness for show tunes when he recorded *What Is This Thing Called Love?* in 1938. The piece demands attention at the start and keeps demanding it all the way through—by alternating minor- and major-key passages, pitting brasses against reeds, giving sturdy parts to the soloists. The full clarinet chorus is bold, the short trumpet passage is clear. The rhythm is pronounced until it—and everything else—stops in one of those abrupt cutoffs that Shaw frequently used. After things start up again, the saxes trip daintily, the trombone plods and the clarinet plays eloquently alone against the tom-toms.

Shaw's arranger, Jerry Gray, gave a brisk character to Cole Porter's brooding song. A world traveler who used to pick up musical ideas in Caribbean villages and South Sea islands, Porter found the basis for *What Is This Thing Called Love?* in a chant he heard in a marketplace in Marrakech.

Band 3 THE DIPSY DOODLE
Tommy Dorsey version

This was an era of silly songs—*The Music Goes 'Round and Around* ("whoa-ho-ho-ho-ho-ho and it comes out here"); *The Flat Foot Floogie* ("with the floy floy"); *Three Little Fishes* ("Down in the meddy, in an itty bitty poo, Fam fee itty fitty and a mamma fitty foo"); *Mairzy Doats* ("and dozy doats and liddle lamzy divey"). *The Dipsy Doodle* was a little more literate than the others, but it didn't make any more sense. Larry Clinton, who —like so many swing era musicians—was a baseball fanatic, got his idea for this song from a left-handed pitcher he admired, Carl Hubbell of the New York Giants. Hubbell had a screwball pitch that had been dubbed the "dipsy doo" for the crazy way it dipped over the plate and befuddled a whole generation of batters.

Clinton at the time was working as an arranger and hanging out nights at the Onyx Club, a jazz joint on 52nd Street, where the backs of the menus were printed with blank music scores. One night Larry scribbled a tune on the menu, but it wasn't until the baseball season started a little later that he found his inspiration for the lyrics.

Clinton used *The Dipsy Doodle* as the theme for the band he later formed. It is an innocent little tune, and Dorsey gave it a good-natured treatment. But its innocence, like that of any good nonsense song, is deceptive. Play it a couple of times, and you'll find yourself going around muttering things like "the moon jumped over the cow hey diddle."

Bands 4 SING, SING, SING   Parts I and II
and 5 *Benny Goodman version*

This Swing Era landmark number started out unpretentiously as a song by Louis Prima. "I was out at the race track back in 1936 with Bing Crosby and George Raft," Prima says. "On the way home the phrase 'Sing, Bing, Sing' kept running through my mind. By the time I got home, I decided that wasn't very commercial and I changed it to 'Sing, Sing, Sing.' " Prima tried it out that night at the Hollywood spot where he was playing trumpet with a small combo. "It got no reaction, but a few days later my publisher brought Benny Goodman around to hear it. Benny was reluctant, but he bought it."

Benny played it first in an arrangement by Jimmy Mundy with a Helen Ward vocal. But as Goodman's men repeated it in the ballrooms and theaters, they began extending some solos and interpolating bits of *Christopher Columbus*. Pretty soon *Sing, Sing, Sing* had merged with *Christopher Columbus*. In July 1937 Goodman recorded this new long version on two sides of a twelve-inch record.

By this time the piece had assumed the strength and dimension of a small concerto—an exciting succession of solos and ensembles bridged by brilliant passages from the drums, especially the tom-toms. The tom-toms start it off, the brass comes in heavily, and the saxophones introduce the theme. The clarinet has a few measures and the tom-toms come back. Saxes and trombones bring on *Christopher Columbus* with trumpets shrieking. It is tom-toms again, with the brass riffing and the reeds repeating a two-note link, and then a long drum solo. As the trumpets play, the drums vary the rhythmic pattern. The clarinet flickers in and the drums subtly change patterns again, setting up a brighter passage for the ensemble.

Part II opens with tom-toms and a dark tenor sax. Another flicker from the clarinet, the ensemble answering. A general wailing and growling follows while drums pound on. The trumpet and the drums carry on a crisp dialogue. A modulation by the trumpet into an ensemble passage and the clarinet is in once more playing short phrases in the low register, soaring and dipping over the tom-toms. The persistent tom-toms rumble softly, then a cowbell gives the signal for the band to sing out a strident end.

Sing, Sing, Sing was the sensation of Goodman's 1938 Carnegie concert, the first swing concert held in that hallowed hall. And—for better or for worse—Gene Krupa's performance popularized the drum as an extended swing solo instrument. But though dozens of drummers decided that if Gene could play solos so could they, few had his flair or irrepressible spirit.

SIDE THREE
Band 1 JOHN'S IDEA
Count Basie version

The John of *John's Idea* is not to be confused with the John of *Big John's Special*, a Benny Goodman number re-created in the 1938-39 album of THE SWING ERA. Both men were benefactors of swing musicians, though in different ways. Big John ran a Harlem gin mill and, as related previously in these notes, befriended sidemen and fed them bean soup. The John of this Basie number was John Hammond, the jazz enthusiast and record producer who financed and furthered the careers of scores of jazz musicians, including Basie.

"John used to like fiery little riffs," recalls Eddie Durham. "He heard this and liked it, so we named it after him." The full title was *I May Be Wrong But It's John's Idea*. In it Basie paid Hammond tribute on his piano, the instrument that has always been the center of the Count's band. It has served as solo instrument, as part of the rhythm section and as the band's pacesetter. Frequently at the start of a piece, wrote the critic Hugues Panassié, "Basie himself hunts for the exact tempo. . . . When the rhythm section joins in, it takes up this perfect tempo, and, by the time the rest of the orchestra comes in, the tempo is already solidly established and it is impossible for anyone to vacillate."

It happens this way in *John's Idea*. The piano takes the introduction (based on the ubiquitous *Christopher Columbus* figure which shows up in several numbers in this album) over cymbal and bass. It attacks the first solo in a sparse and swinging style, then playfully picks up some mannerisms of the great Fats Waller—thirds in triplets and descending left-hand octaves. The band takes up the idea and, after a tenor sax chorus (originally by Herschel Evans), climbs dramatically up the scale in seven half steps, tossing the eighth to the piano. There is some more Waller and, after some brass riffing, the piano ripples through a series of graceful runs before the ensemble's closing crescendo.

It is interesting to hear, in the three Basie re-creations played in this SWING ERA album, the variety of Basie's styles. In *John's Idea* he showed a classical command of the jazz piano. In *Blue and Sentimental* (Side 2) he played what could almost be cocktail-lounge piano except that he never dropped into clichés. And in *Every Tub* (Side 1) he made almost as much music with the notes he didn't play as with those he did. In another band, so masterful a pianist might have overpowered everybody else. But, like his piano-playing colleague Duke Ellington, Basie knew when enough was enough. "My piano?" Basie has commented. "I love to play, but this idea of one man taking one chorus after another is not wise. I fed dancers my own piano in short doses, and when I came in for a solo, I did it unexpectedly, using a strong rhythm behind me. That way we figure the Count's piano wasn't going to get monotonous."

Band 2 COQUETTE
Jimmie Lunceford version

Precocious Johnny Green composed his first song when he was four years old, but that seemed to be only a flash in a pan. Years went by, and he was all of eighteen before he got a piece published. He wrote it when he was a junior at Harvard, and the next summer, when he was working as a boy-wonder arranger for Guy Lombardo, he had Guy's brother Carmen help him fix it up. Carmen got the lyricist Gus Kahn to provide the words. The lyrics are vintage syrup, but the tune has character; and the Lunceford band, taking it slow and easy, generates a good deal of heat. The muted trumpets of the opening chorus are set against some unexpected harmonies and accents. The tenor sax keeps things moving. Dan Grissom, who was a star singer for Lunceford, lends a period authenticity here by singing the vocal again for this re-creation.

Green went back to finish at Harvard, and by the time he was halfway through his senior year, *Coquette* had become a hit. Green has gone on, of course, to write many hits (*Body and Soul, I Cover the Waterfront*)—none, he says today, more satisfyingly successful than his first.

Band 3 LIZA
Chick Webb version

Few songs had so auspicious an introduction to Broadway as *Liza*. It was written by George Gershwin in 1929 for Florenz Ziegfeld's *Show Girl* and was sung by Ruby Keeler, the pert young song-and-dance girl who had just married Al Jolson. On opening night in New York, after Ruby had sung *Liza*, her newly wed husband stood up at his seat in the theater and, in the voice that had made so many songs famous, sang a second chorus. The audience was ecstatic, and the *New York Times* remarked that "it was a touching episode"—unaware, apparently, that Jolson had done this same impromptu bit at the Boston tryout and was so pleased by the effect that he decided to do it again on Broadway.

The song itself didn't need all that help—it is Gershwin at his most appealing. Chick Webb's arrangement was written by Benny Carter, and it is regarded by swing musicologists as a classic. It gives the solo prominence to the drums but has much more in it—expert ensemble phrasing, agile work from the saxophones and a chorus in which the brass soloists shine: first the zinging trumpet, then the strong trombone, then the trumpet back again.

Liza was one of Webb's favorite pieces in the days when he ruled over the Savoy Ballroom in Harlem and lured anybody and everybody into battles of jazz. "Any visiting band could depend on catching hell from little Chick," said Mary Lou Williams, the pianist-composer, "for he was a crazy drummer and shrewd to boot. Chick would wait until the opposition had blown its hottest numbers and then, during a so-so set, would unexpectedly bring his band fresh to the stand and wham into a fine arrangement, like Benny Carter's *Liza*, that was hard to beat. Few bands could stand up to this."

Band 4 NIGHTMARE
Artie Shaw version

"We called it *Nightmare*," said Artie Shaw, giving one of his explanations that didn't explain anything, "because we had to call it something." Tony Pastor, who used to play saxophone for Shaw, is more informative. "One night up in a Boston hotel," he says, "Artie started noodling around with this tune and it sounded just like a nightmare." The passage that Artie noodled is set off in *Nightmare* by a foreboding figure which, says Harry Rodgers, Shaw's old trombonist, "comes from Stravinsky's *Firebird*, about a third of the way through the dance of the Princess— a peaceful little thing, but Artie put a screaming thing with it." The figure, three notes ascending and descending, moves gloomily throughout the piece. After the wailing trumpets, the clarinet appears briefly, then returns for a beautifully fashioned solo. Artie liked the number. When he had to pick a theme song at short notice for a broadcast, he chose *Nightmare*, and the uneasy number came to identify one of the most self-assured bands of its time.

Band 5 MARCH OF THE BOB CATS
Bob Crosby version

It seems a long way from *O Tannenbaum* to *March of the Bob Cats*, but with a little patience the genealogy can be untangled. The familiar old German melody probably began as a Catholic hymn and had become a Christmas carol by the time it was brought to America by German immigrants. In 1861, when Secessionist mobs in Baltimore attacked Union troops, a young Marylander named James Ryder Randall, who was teaching school in New Orleans, hailed their action with a fiery verse that began: "Dear Mother! Burst the tyrant's chain, Maryland my Maryland." Back in Baltimore, Jenny and Hetty Cary, a pair of noted beauties, read the poem in a newspaper and, at a musicale they gave for a group of Southern sympathizers, Jenny sang the words to the tune of *Tannenbaum*. (Actually, she didn't know *Tannenbaum* but did know a college song called *Lauriger Horatius* which was derived from *Tannenbaum*.) *Maryland* became a Confederate favorite and, later, a standard piece for New Orleans marching bands. When the marching bands became the first jazz bands, they still played it. Zutty Singleton, the drummer, remembers seeing Louis Armstrong when he was a boy, "playing in a band at a picnic. He was playing *Maryland, My Maryland* and he sure was swinging out that melody."

In 1938 the eight Crosby Bob Cats scheduled *Maryland* at a recording session. "We liked to take tired old war horses," says Crosby, "and give them a rambunctious two-beat. But the president of the record company came in the studio and said: 'You can't jazz up that immortal song. It's sacrilege.' So we waited until he went out, and then we took the chord structure and changed the melody and called it *March of the Bob Cats*."

By any name, *March of the Bob Cats* is still *Maryland, My Maryland*. A snare drum summons the ensemble. A clarinet yodels around the melody. A milky tenor sax takes a short solo, the horns march back in, and everybody joins a high-stepping chorus full of Dixieland riffs and an ebullience that no record producer could suppress.

Band 1 BACK BAY SHUFFLE
Artie Shaw version

Teddy McRae was playing tenor sax in 1938 with Chick Webb at a night spot in Boston next to the Roseland where Artie Shaw was appearing. "Artie used to come in and listen to us," McRae remembers. "He was young and just getting started, and one night he asked if I could do some instrumentals for him. I told him, half as a joke, that I'd have a big hit for him when I got back next weekend. In those days, everything closed down tight in Boston on Sunday and, when they'd finished on Saturday night, all the musicians would rush for the 1:05 train to New York. The saxes in *Back Bay Shuffle* play the sounds we used to hear of the wheels coming around the bend as we dashed for the train in Back Bay Station."

Catchy and tongue in cheek, *Back Bay Shuffle* is full of things that distinguished Shaw's first successful band—the one that he himself has always liked most of all his bands. The beat is firm and light; the sections bend the notes; the soloists play with contrasting textures. The clarinet comes whistling in and scampers around the melody. The trombone lets go. The trumpet blows an impish reminder of Bix Beiderbecke's famous chorus in *Riverboat Shuffle*. After the piano enjoys a solo, the sections answer each other, leaving a little time for the tenor sax and the hint of a bumps-and-grind routine. Throughout the concoction, the band is driven along by the steady drums. These were played originally by Cliff Leeman, one of swing's less showy drummers but a musician cherished by sidemen for the way he kept them going without ever getting in their way.

Band 2 SMOKE RINGS
Glen Gray version

There were no sounds in all swing so haunting as the high muted trombone and clarinets that open *Smoke Rings* and the solo clarinet that comes in with a trill to float over the rhythm, singing, spiraling, dissolving. *Smoke Rings* was the Casa Loma's theme—and the most original theme song of its time. Gene Gifford, the band's composer-arranger, may have written it in a few minutes, as related on page 44 of this volume. But it is a thoughtfully arranged work. The combination of trombone and clarinets at the start was a jazz innovation, and the way the band comes to a crescendo at the end of every four bars in the third chorus is a little lesson in how to get drama out of a succession of on-the-beat chords.

"*Smoke Rings*," says Larry Clinton, who was an arranger for Casa Loma before he formed his own band, "was the first jazz piece outside the blues that was so slow—most jazz pieces were basically upbeat. This one did not depend on jazz rhythm or beat. It was jazz because of its chord structure, and the arrangement gave the solo artist freedom to move within its bounds."

The soloist who took advantage of this freedom was an untrammeled spirit named Clarence Hutchenrider, the Casa Loma's clarinetist. In a band that prized group effort and never encouraged soloists, Hutch modestly but firmly established himself as one of the finest solo sidemen of his time. His tone was ravishing, his technique clean, his ornamentation rich and almost florid. Hutch still plays in New York and, he says, "almost every night someone asks me to play *Smoke Rings*, and I always do. I still have a feeling for the song—never seem to get tired of it."

Band 3 LITTLE ROCK GETAWAY
Bob Crosby version

Pianist Joe Sullivan has memorialized in music some of the landmarks in a jazz career that started in the early Chicago days. His *Gin Mill Blues* (THE SWING ERA, 1936-37 album) recalls the years he played in New York and Chicago speakeasies. His rollicking *Little Rock Getaway* celebrates his first wife's hometown. He met Mary Ann in New York where she was trying to make it in show business. When she gave up and went back to Little Rock to teach school, Joe meandered after her and they got married.

The Crosby band added *Little Rock Getaway* to its "book" during the three months Sullivan played with Crosby in 1937 and recorded it, after tuberculosis had forced Sullivan into temporary retirement, with Bob Zurke at the keyboard. Joe always liked Little Rock, where he says the folks treated him wonderfully, and the music makes it sound like a joyous place. Sullivan set the piece in ragtime, and the Crosby band was cheerily faithful to its spirit. The piano opens in a familiar ragtime way, tinkling down the scales in the right hand and striding up the scale in the left. The piano leaves to let a tenor sax have a full chorus, but it gets back, runs through variations and scoots off, ragging as it goes.

Band 4 I CAN'T GET STARTED
Bunny Berigan version

To everybody in the 1930s, this was Bunny Berigan's song—to everybody, that is, except Bob Hope. "In 1936," Hope wrote in his autobiography, "I landed in the 'Ziegfeld Follies'. For me the big thing was that I was introduced to *I Can't Get Started*. I picked out a big beautiful redhead show gal to sing it to—Eve Arden. When I began to warble, she walked away. I followed, leaned over her shoulder and breathed deeply with unrequited passion. When I sang 'I can't get started' the people didn't believe it. The first four rows could hear my motor running."

The song did a lot for Hope, helping him land his first movie job. But what did more for the song than anything or anyone else was the trumpet of Roland Bernard Berigan, re-created here by Shorty Sherock. It starts with a passage that is as arresting in its own way as the classic cadenza which opens Louis Armstrong's *West End Blues*. With a strong, velvety tone, it blows through an astonishing octave range, ending on a beautifully shaded high note and sweeping into the first chorus. The trumpet is hot but has a lyric roundness. It speaks with a full voice, then drops into a whisper. It breaks into cleanly accented variations, climbs up without a quaver or a squeak, drops into a subdued low-register passage, then gradually goes back up to a high C sharp of triumph. (No attempt has been made in this recording to re-create Berigan's vocal.)

This rueful torch song mirrors Berigan's career. A hard-living, softhearted man, he had learned music in Fox Lake, Wisconsin, playing violin and trumpet in his grandfather's orchestra. Artie Shaw remembers him in New York in the late '20s "flat broke like most of the rest of us, trying to find himself any little job so he could earn some kind of living with his trumpet."

Soon the jobs came easily—with Rudy Vallee, Hal Kemp, Paul Whiteman. By late 1933 Bunny was moving in hotter jazz circles. In the following years he lent his brilliance to Benny Goodman and to Tommy Dorsey for a series of notable recordings. His was the trumpet in Goodman's *King Porter Stomp* and *Blue Skies* and in Dorsey's *Marie* and *Song of India*. In 1937 he formed his own band and, with *I Can't Get Started* and *Prisoner's Song*, was a modest success.

But Berigan burned his strength and talent away in work and drink. In 1942, warned by doctors that playing the trumpet any more would kill him, he played anyway. He was only thirty-three when he died. "Bunny was a true musician," said saxophonist Bud Freeman. "He loved music and he loved people. But you have to be tough to get along in the band business and he hated the music business."

Band 5 QUAKER CITY JAZZ
Jan Savitt version

If anybody harbored the idea that Philadelphia was a slow place, he would be disabused on hearing Jan Savitt play his theme song, *Quaker City Jazz*. It gets off in nervous haste with clanging cymbals, muttering trombones, punching trumpets and a trombone trilling rapidly in the high register. It keeps going prestissimo through the brass work, the mile-a-minute alto solo, and the rapid riffs until you wonder how anybody had any breath left to play those whomping last chords.

It was from this number and from a style called the "shuffle beat" that Jan Savitt gained fame—and fame was what he was always after. A Russian-born violinist who studied to become a symphony conductor, Savitt made a modest name for himself conducting a radio-studio band in Philadelphia. The job kept him tied down, and when a chance came to play in New York, he grabbed it, even though he had to leave most of his musicians behind. "Jan was a short man and always wanted to be a big man," recalls Savitt's trumpeter, Jack Hansen. "When I first joined him, the men appeared in top hat and tails, and Savitt wore a cape and top hat. He always carried on this way. There was something of Napoleon about him—with style."

SIDE FIVE
Band 1 FOR DANCERS ONLY
Jimmie Lunceford version

Nothing gives a swing musician more satisfaction than pointing out how wrong-headed record producers can be. Artie Shaw has gloated for years over the fact that the record people didn't want to make *Begin the Beguine*. And Sy Oliver still remembers scornfully that "the brilliant officials at Decca refused to record *For Dancers Only*. They said it wasn't Lunceford, and it was only after another band came out with an imitation that caught on that they let us make it."

No song, of course, has been more thoroughly identified with Lunceford than *For Dancers Only* with its earthy, elemental sound and its heavy but never ponderous beat. "All the melodic lines in it," Oliver explains, "were things the guys in the band played all the time. It was a sort of compilation of riffs." The first one is the emphatic figure made familiar in *Christopher Columbus*. The trumpets push into it, over some raucous pedal tones from the trombones. Then a short sax solo takes it, with variations and whinnies. The trumpets launch one of their section on a high-note solo. All through, the saxophones keep busy—shaking, smearing, riffing.

The skill of the sax section, admired everywhere in the business, could be traced to Willie Smith, alto sax player and section leader. Willie always claimed that he was not a black but an Egyptian—and he looked like one. He was also a first-class eccentric. "He always had to be the last man on the stand," recalls Trummy Young, Lunceford's trombonist, "and usually got up there terribly late to be sure he was last. He also had to be the last man off the stand and would stay there all through intermission if one of the guys tried to put him on and wait him out. He had his own way of lighting matches and a ritual in putting the mouthpiece on his saxophone—three turns, no more, no less. He had tremendous talent. Every good alto solo was always attributed to Willie even when he didn't play it. This discouraged the other guys. But he was loved by everybody in the band and everybody was influenced by Willie."

Band 2 MUSIC, MAESTRO, PLEASE!
Tommy Dorsey version

"Herb Magidson and I wrote this over a Ping-Pong table," says Allie Wrubel, explaining *Music, Maestro, Please!* Wrubel, who also composed such hits as *Zip-a Dee Doo-Dah* and *As You Desire Me*, and Magidson, who wrote lyrics for *The Continental* and *I'll Dance at Your Wedding*, were neighbors as well as collaborators in California in the 1930s. When they got together for work in the mornings, they would warm up with a little Ping-Pong. "We started out with the title on *Music, Maestro* and we batted the ball back and forth, the lyrics back and forth and the tune back and forth, and by the time we had played one game, the song was as good as written."

Tommy Dorsey gave it the medium-tempo treatment that he did almost better than anyone else—one reason the music popularity polls kept choosing him as a winner in both the swing and sweet band categories. The muted trombone sings the melody straight over smooth saxes and a gentle trumpet. The ensemble plays lightly behind the vocalist, and the tenor sax blows a pretty four bars toward the end.

"*Music* was a big hit all over the world," says Magidson and adds a macabre note: "Somebody even committed suicide to it. A guy jumped off a bridge in Pittsburgh, and the cops who were trying to get to him heard him singing *Music, Maestro, Please!* as he jumped."

Band 3 POWERHOUSE
Raymond Scott version

Raymond Scott found his inspiration for *Powerhouse* right next door—when he was rehearsing in a studio on West 53rd Street in New York next to an electrical generating plant. Curious about the sounds he heard coming from the plant, Scott stepped inside one day and came out with a musical idea and, just as important to him, a title. The number does conjure up something electrical—cymbals beating, sticks batting, brass buzzing, tenor sax and clarinet going in unison at about 50,000 r.p.m. Suddenly, the power is cut off and, with the sound of a ticking clock, the quintet lapses into a more conventional interlude. But the power comes on again and the piece buzzes to the end. The xylophone notes in the interlude, incidentally, were played on the smallest xylophone ever used professionally. "We needed only six or seven notes," Scott explains, "so we took just the notes we needed from a full xylophone, put them on a little wooden mounting, and, when it came time, the trumpeter would put his trumpet under his arm, pick up the wooden mount and, holding it with one hand, would play it with the other."

Band 4 I LET A SONG GO OUT OF MY HEART
Duke Ellington version

All the musicianship that Duke Ellington could put into his songs—and that his band could get out of them—can be heard in *I Let a Song Go Out of My Heart*. There is an edge to the sweet harmonies, and there is steam behind the easy beat. But the most memorable part comes early when two saxophones join in a chorus, the rich-sounding baritone taking a melody while the alto does a playful obbligato. This was played originally by a pair of sidemen who grew up together in Boston, Johnny Hodges and Harry Carney. Benny Goodman, a man usually sparing in his praise, called Hodges "by far the greatest man on alto sax that I ever heard" and added that "bashful Harry Carney" is "just about the same on baritone sax." Carney never achieved Hodges' popular fame, but among musicians he has been the acknowledged master of his bulky, thick-voiced saxophone. From an instrument which once was called upon to provide funny raspy noises or deep boop-boops, Carney draws an astonishingly dulcet tone and moves with supple ease up and down its scale.

Carney was playing clarinet and alto sax when he joined Ellington more than forty years ago. He and another newcomer to the band were competing for the "hot" clarinet chair. "Lots of times during the evening you would hear nothing but clarinets from the reed section," Carney told Stanley Dance, author of *The World of Duke Ellington*, "so I decided to try baritone. . . . Duke and everyone seemed to think it was quite good. My greatest kick with the instrument, which then seemed so much bigger than me, was that I was able to fill it and make some noise with it." Bashful Harry still plays with Ellington today. "There was always something going on in the band," he explains. "I guess that's why I always stayed with Duke. He was always experimenting, and I liked the way he thought about music. I was always surprised when fellows left the band."

SIDE SIX
Band 1 BOOGIE WOOGIE
Tommy Dorsey version

In its early days, boogie-woogie was played at rent-party dances in Chicago's black ghetto by Pinetop Smith, who gave the music its name and who, before he died in 1929 in a dance-hall brawl, left behind a superb record called *Pinetop's Boogie Woogie*. On it Pinetop not only played piano but also called out instructions like some South Side square-dance caller. Pinetop's piano begins the number with the now-familiar boogie tremolo and takes a chorus. Then his voice breaks in with:

"Listen now, all of you, this is my Pinetop strut."	*(the piano starts a second chorus)*
"I want everybody dancin' just like I tell you."	*(the piano keeps going)*
"And when I say hold yourself, everybody get ready to stop."	*(emphasis in the left hand)*
"And when I say stop, don't move a thing."	*(the bass keeps rolling)*
"And when I say git it, everybody do a boogie-woogie."	*(the right hand goes up)*
"Hold yourself now."	*(right-hand tremolo and a commanding passage down the scale)*
"Boogie-Woogie!"	*(the piano rolls)*
"When I say git it, everybody mess around."	
"Hold yourself."	*(right hand tremolo)*
"Mess around."	*(and the piano swings away)*

In arranging this pioneering piece, Deane Kincaide, who played saxophone for Tommy Dorsey, caught the light swing that graced Pinetop's playing—and was lost by some of his heavy-handed followers. The piano plays the boogie straight, the soloists and sections share the figures and not until a mournful trombone (originally Dorsey) blows in does the band depart—only briefly—from the patterns Pinetop set. "Tommy made about $100,000 all told on *Boogie Woogie*," says Kincaide. "I got twenty bucks for the arrangement and another twenty-five playing the first record date."

Band 2 TWILIGHT IN TURKEY
Raymond Scott version

"I've always liked combinations of words," confesses Raymond Scott, "and when I had my Quintet, I was always looking for words I could write music about. One day, going through a newspaper, I saw the word 'Turkey' and then a couple of pages later I saw 'twilight.' I liked the sound of them together." What came from this alliteration was an ingenious exercise in instrumentation. The opening is drums, joined by the bass. While the sax and clarinet run an arpeggio, the trumpet buzzes underneath. Sax, clarinet and trumpet do a sweet trio, the drum a long solo. The muted trumpet and clarinet interpolate an Oriental melody while the drummer clinks with a pair of finger cymbals—tiny versions of the big brass disks slipped on the thumb and one finger. The tenor sax whips a fast solo, winding up on a trill, and the horns take the piece out as it came in.

The only thing remotely Turkish about *Twilight in Turkey* is the familiar melody halfway through. "If I were going to write about Turkey," explains Scott, "I had to have an Oriental theme. When I was growing up, anybody who would do a belly dance would always hum the theme I used. I guess it must be the most notorious phrase in the history of music." Where the theme originally came from, nobody seems to know—whether from snake charmers, oasis swingers, or Mideastern folk singers. It did show up in a song called *The Streets of Cairo* or *Poor Little Country Girl*, written in 1893 by a famous old music hall performer named James Thornton. It told about a girl who came to the Chicago's World's Fair and never got to see the Streets of Cairo, the sideshow where Little Egypt danced. Once a barbershop quartet favorite, the song is now long forgotten. But the melody lingers on, kept alive by generations of kids who, feeling very naughty about it, have sung it with the words: "Oh, they wear no pants, In the hootchy-kootchy dance" (or, sometimes, ". . . In the sunny south of France").

Band 3 MARGIE
Jimmie Lunceford version

Margie has had quite a career. It was written by Con Conrad and J. Russel Robinson to honor Eddie Cantor's five-year-old daughter. Eddie sang it on Broadway, of course. *Margie* was one of the first jazz-record best sellers—the one the Original Dixieland Jazz Band made in 1920 with *Palesteena* on the other side.

Of all the hundreds of *Margies* sung and played since then, none stands up to the one Jimmie Lunceford recorded in 1938. This is partly because of Sy Oliver's swinging arrangement, partly because of the expressive alto sax solo but mostly because of the wonderfully infectious choruses sung and played by Trummy Young, vocalist and trombonist, who came back to re-create in this SWING ERA album the solos he did more than thirty years ago.

Band 5 CHANGES
Benny Goodman version

A special dancing delight seemed to take over the Goodman band when it played the old 1920s hit, *Changes*. It begins with bouncing brass and doodling reeds and goes into one of the happiest passages in the whole Goodman repertory— soft saxes playing lilting variations while trumpets build bright tone pyramids. A trumpet comes on strong over a heavy beat, but the saxes push it aside. Then the clarinet wings off with the melody, tossing off a trill as it goes.

Changes was composed by Walter Donaldson (*My Blue Heaven, My Mammy, At Sundown*) and arranged by Fletcher Henderson. "I remember," says Gene Krupa, Goodman's drummer, "that we used to listen to a Bix Beiderbecke record of *Changes* made with Paul Whiteman. Bix had about half a chorus for a solo, which was something in those days. I guess that's one reason we liked the song so much."

He reminisced about how he came to do the song: "I always liked that tune since I was a child, and once I told Sy Oliver I'd been kind of thinking about it and I hummed it for him. I must have hummed my version of it five or six times, and he kept filling in the skeleton of the background. *Margie* was the first vocal I ever did—it was one of the only tunes I knew the lyrics to—and was it ever popular! Every girl named Margie thought I was singing it for her."

He sings it here in his wispy voice, then takes it on his trombone in a solo that winds up in a fabulous light glissando. "Trummy's trombone break on the last chorus," says Sy Oliver, "is very high and very difficult. I don't remember how many takes we did in making that record in 1938—maybe eight or nine —and on all the takes, Trummy never missed that break once."

Trummy had learned to play the trombone at military school—not because he liked music, but "if you were in the band you got out of some of the drilling and anything was better than drilling." He used to listen endlessly to Louis Armstrong records and try to copy on his trombone the solos Louis did on the trumpet. By the time he was fourteen he was playing professionally, and in 1933 he joined Earl Hines at the Grand Terrace in Chicago. By 1937, several bands were after him. "I could have gone to Cab Calloway for twice as much as Lunceford," he once explained, "but I couldn't stand all that hollerin'. . . . Lunceford warned me I was coming into a nice band. They were all educated, well-behaved fellows, he said—some even went to church and Sunday school regularly. I told him I wasn't well educated, sometimes a little wild. I didn't go to church and wasn't figuring to start it, and he'd hired me to play trombone in that Sunday-school band. Man, I was the ignorant one in that band. . . . It was a punctual outfit. Nothing haphazard. But it had wonderful spirit. We never made much, but it sure was fun playing."

Band 4 ROLL 'EM
Benny Goodman version

Mary Lou Williams was paying tribute to another pianist in this number: her Kansas City colleague Pete Johnson who, whenever he began a boogie-woogie, would be greeted by cries of "Roll 'em, Pete" from his admirers. The first three choruses are straight instrumental boogie, and the piano solo (played in the original by Jess Stacy) takes up the boogie beat—but just for a few measures. Almost immediately it evolves into a swinging 4/4 with a strong left-hand stride and an arching trumpet-style treble. There is very little boogie left, just plain old blues, when the clarinet comes on, brightening as it goes, and the trumpet—originally one of Harry James's finest solos with Goodman—moves up out of the middle into the high and higher registers. But before the piece ends, the ensemble brings the boogie-woogie back.

Band 5 SOUTH RAMPART STREET PARADE
Bob Crosby version

Street names have furnished titles for many classic jazz pieces: *Beale Street Blues* (New Orleans), *Twelfth Street Rag* (Kansas City), and *Basin Street Blues* and *Bourbon Street Blues* (both New Orleans). South Rampart Street is in New Orleans, too, and Ray Bauduc, drummer in Bob Crosby's band, remembers that when he was a boy, "it was a main drag in the colored section, full of fancy men's clothing stores, saloons and pawnshops. During Mardi Gras, the carnival bands started marching at the Basin, where the King of Zulu lands. They'd come strutting up South Rampart, play a fanfare and swing into Claiborne."

He was describing this scene one night at a New York hotel date to Bob Haggart, the band's bassist and arranger, who was nursing an intermission drink at a table. Ray hummed a marching tune to Haggart and said, "Put this down." Haggart obligingly took out his pen and started scribbling notes on the only handy writing material, the tablecloth. He remembered to take the cloth home with him that night and, under the nagging of Bauduc, finally finished *South Rampart Street Parade*.

The piece sounds more marched than played—with the brass and reeds competing, the low-voiced trombones and the high-voiced trumpets, the fancy-stepping counter melodies and the liquid clarinet, and the whole band strutting into the finale in a great old Dixieland style, half martial and half Mardi Gras.

—JOSEPH KASTNER

The Musicians Who Made the Recordings in This Volume

DON'T BE THAT WAY
LEADER: Billy May TRUMPETS: Shorty Sherock, John Audino, Uan Rasey TROMBONES: Lloyd Ulyate, Dick Noel SAXOPHONES: Skeets Herfurt, Willie Schwartz, Justin Gordon, Plas Johnson PIANO: Ray Sherman GUITAR: Jack Marshall BASS: Rolly Bundock DRUMS: Nick Fatool SOLOS: Lew McCreary (trombone), Joe Graves (trumpet), Abe Most (clarinet)

SLEEPY TIME GAL
LEADER: Billy May TRUMPETS: Pete Candoli, John Best, Uan Rasey TROMBONES: Joe Howard, Lew McCreary, Lloyd Ulyate, Dick Nash SAXOPHONES: Les Robinson, Willie Schwartz, Justin Gordon, Don Raffell, Jack Nimitz PIANO: Ray Sherman GUITAR: Jack Marshall BASS: Rolly Bundock DRUMS: Nick Fatool SOLOS: Abe Most (clarinet), Dick Nash (trombone)

ANNIE LAURIE
LEADER: Billy May TRUMPETS: Pete Candoli, Shorty Sherock, John Best TROMBONES: Joe Howard, Lew McCreary, Dick Nash SAXOPHONES: Les Robinson, Justin Gordon, Abe Most, Don Lodice, Chuck Gentry PIANO: Ray Sherman GUITAR: Jack Marshall BASS: Rolly Bundock DRUMS: Nick Fatool SOLOS: Don Lodice (tenor saxophone), Trummy Young (trombone)

SUMMERTIME
LEADER: Glen Gray TRUMPETS: Conrad Gozzo, Shorty Sherock, Frank Beach, Uan Rasey TROMBONES: Joe Howard, Ed Kusby, Milt Bernhart, Lew McCreary SAXOPHONES: Abe Most, Skeets Herfurt, Julie Jacob, Chuck Gentry, Plas Johnson PIANO: Ray Sherman GUITAR: Jack Marshall BASS: Mike Rubin DRUMS: Nick Fatool SOLO: Plas Johnson (tenor saxophone)

EVERY TUB
LEADER: Billy May TRUMPETS: Shorty Sherock, John Best, Uan Rasey TROMBONES: Joe Howard, Dick Nash, Lew McCreary SAXOPHONES: Les Robinson, Justin Gordon, Abe Most, Don Raffell PIANO: Ray Sherman

GUITAR: Jack Marshall BASS: Rolly Bundock DRUMS: Nick Fatool SOLOS: Pete Candoli (trumpet), Don Raffell (opening and closing tenor saxophone solos), Justin Gordon (second tenor saxophone solo)

BLUE AND SENTIMENTAL
LEADER: Billy May TRUMPETS: Pete Candoli, Shorty Sherock, Uan Rasey TROMBONES: Joe Howard, Lew McCreary, Lloyd Ulyate SAXOPHONES: Willie Schwartz, Abe Most, Justin Gordon, Plas Johnson PIANO: Ray Sherman GUITAR: Jack Marshall BASS: Rolly Bundock DRUMS: Nick Fatool SOLOS: Plas Johnson (tenor saxophone), Shorty Sherock (trumpet), Abe Most (clarinet)

WHAT IS THIS THING CALLED LOVE?
LEADER: Billy May TRUMPETS: John Audino, Uan Rasey, Shorty Sherock, Ray Triscari TROMBONES: Lew McCreary, Lloyd Ulyate, Joe Howard SAXOPHONES: Les Robinson, Willie Schwartz, Justin Gordon, Julie Jacob PIANO: Ray Sherman GUITAR: Jack Marshall BASS: Rolly Bundock DRUMS: Nick Fatool SOLOS: Abe Most (clarinet), Shorty Sherock (trumpet), Lloyd Ulyate (trombone)

THE DIPSY DOODLE
LEADER: Billy May TRUMPETS: Pete Candoli, Shorty Sherock, Uan Rasey TROMBONES: Joe Howard, Dick Nash, Lew McCreary SAXOPHONES: Les Robinson, Justin Gordon, Abe Most, Don Raffell PIANO: Ray Sherman GUITAR: Jack Marshall BASS: Rolly Bundock DRUMS: Nick Fatool VOCAL: Eileen Wilson

SING, SING, SING: PART I
LEADER: Billy May TRUMPETS: Pete Candoli, John Audino, Shorty Sherock, Uan Rasey TROMBONES: Lew McCreary, Dick Noel SAXOPHONES: Skeets Herfurt, Willie Schwartz, Justin Gordon, Plas Johnson PIANO: Ray Sherman GUITAR: Jack Marshall BASS: Mike Rubin DRUMS: Nick Fatool SOLO: Abe Most (clarinet)

SING, SING, SING: PART II
LEADER: Billy May TRUMPETS: Pete Candoli, John Audino, Shorty Sherock, Uan Rasey TROMBONES: Lloyd Ulyate, Dick Noel SAXOPHONES: Skeets Herfurt, Willie Schwartz, Justin Gordon, Plas Johnson PIANO: Ray Sherman GUITAR: Jack Marshall BASS: Mike Rubin DRUMS: Nick Fatool SOLOS: Joe Graves (trumpet), Plas Johnson (tenor saxophone)

JOHN'S IDEA
LEADER: Billy May TRUMPETS: Pete Candoli, John Best, Uan Rasey TROMBONES: Dick Nash, Lew McCreary SAXOPHONES: Les Robinson, Justin Gordon, Abe Most, Don Raffell PIANO: Ray Sherman GUITAR: Jack Marshall BASS: Rolly Bundock DRUMS: Nick Fatool SOLO: Justin Gordon (tenor saxophone)

COQUETTE
LEADER: Billy May TRUMPETS: Conrad Gozzo, Manny Klein, Ollie Mitchell, Pete Candoli, Vito Mangano TROMBONES: Trummy Young, Ed Kusby, Si Zentner, Dick Noel, Joe Howard SAXOPHONES: Willie Smith, Joe Thomas, Willie Schwartz, Ted Nash, Chuck Gentry, Bob Lawson PIANO: Jimmie Rowles GUITAR: Al Hendrickson BASS: Joe Mondragon DRUMS: Alvin Stoller SOLOS: Joe Thomas (tenor saxophone) VOCAL: Dan Grissom

LIZA
LEADER: Billy May TRUMPETS: Pete Candoli, John Best, Uan Rasey TROMBONES: Joe Howard, Dick Nash, Lloyd Ulyate SAXOPHONES: Les Robinson, Willie Schwartz, Justin Gordon, Don Raffell PIANO: Ray Sherman GUITAR: Jack Marshall BASS: Rolly Bundock DRUMS: Nick Fatool SOLOS: Nick Fatool (drums), Shorty Sherock (trumpet), Lew McCreary (trombone)

NIGHTMARE
LEADER: Glen Gray TRUMPETS: Conrad Gozzo, Shorty Sherock, Joe Graves, Uan Rasey, Manny Klein TROMBONES: Ed Kusby, Joe Howard, Milt Bernhart, Lew McCreary SAXOPHONES: Abe Most, Skeets Herfurt, Justin Gordon, Chuck Gentry, Plas Johnson PIANO: Ray Sherman GUITAR: Jack Marshall BASS: Mike Rubin DRUMS: Nick Fatool SOLO: Abe Most (clarinet)

MARCH OF THE BOB CATS
LEADER: Billy May TRUMPETS: Pete Candoli TROMBONE: Joe Howard CLARINET: Abe Most TENOR SAXOPHONE: Justin Gordon PIANO: Ray Sherman GUITAR: Bob Bain BASS: Rolly Bundock DRUMS: Nick Fatool

BACK BAY SHUFFLE
LEADER: Billy May TRUMPETS: John Audino, Ray Triscari, Uan Rasey TROMBONES: Joe Howard, Lew McCreary, Lloyd Ulyate SAXOPHONES: Les Robinson, Willie Schwartz, Justin Gordon, Julie Jacob PIANO: Ray Sherman GUITAR: Jack Marshall BASS: Rolly Bundock DRUMS: Nick Fatool SOLOS: Abe Most (clarinet), Joe Howard (trombone), Shorty Sherock (trumpet), Ray Sherman (piano), Justin Gordon (tenor saxophone)

SMOKE RINGS
LEADER: Billy May TRUMPETS: Shorty Sherock, Ray Triscari, Uan Rasey TROMBONES: Lew McCreary, Lloyd Ulyate, Joe Howard SAXOPHONES: Les Robinson, Abe Most, Justin Gordon, Julie Jacob PIANO: Ray Sherman GUITAR: Jack Marshall BASS: Rolly Bundock DRUMS: Nick Fatool SOLOS: Joe Howard (trombone), Abe Most (clarinet)

LITTLE ROCK GETAWAY
LEADER: Glen Gray TRUMPETS: Pete Candoli, Conrad Gozzo, Joe Graves, Manny Klein, Shorty Sherock TROMBONES: Milt Bernhart, Joe Howard, Ed Kusby, Dick Noel SAXOPHONES: Gus Bivona, Chuck Gentry, Skeets Herfurt, Julie Jacob, Babe Russin PIANO: Ray Sherman GUITAR: Jack Marshall BASS: Mike Rubin DRUMS: Nick Fatool SOLO: Babe Russin (tenor saxophone)

I CAN'T GET STARTED
LEADER: Glen Gray TRUMPETS: Conrad Gozzo, Shorty Sherock, Joe Graves, Uan Rasey, Manny Klein TROMBONES: Joe Howard, Ed Kusby, Milt Bernhart, Lew McCreary SAXOPHONES: Abe Most, Skeets Herfurt, Babe Russin, Chuck Gentry, Plas Johnson PIANO: Ray Sherman GUITAR: Jack Marshall BASS: Mike Rubin DRUMS: Nick Fatool SOLO: Shorty Sherock (trumpet)

QUAKER CITY JAZZ
LEADER: Glen Gray TRUMPETS: Conrad Gozzo, Shorty Sherock, Joe Graves, Uan Rasey, Manny Klein TROMBONES: Joe Howard, Ed Kusby, Milt Bernhart, Lew McCreary SAXOPHONES: Abe Most, Skeets Herfurt, Babe Russin, Chuck Gentry, Plas Johnson PIANO: Ray Sherman GUITAR: Jack Marshall BASS: Mike Rubin DRUMS: Nick Fatool SOLOS: Ed Kusby (trombone), Skeets Herfurt (alto saxophone), Abe Most (clarinet)

FOR DANCERS ONLY
LEADER: Billy May TRUMPETS: Pete Candoli, Shorty Sherock, John Best, Uan Rasey TROMBONES: Dick Nash, Joe Howard, Lew McCreary SAXOPHONES: Les Robinson, Justin Gordon, Abe Most, Don Lodice, Chuck Gentry PIANO: Ray Sherman GUITAR: Jack Marshall BASS: Rolly Bundock DRUMS: Nick Fatool SOLOS: Les Robinson (alto saxophone), Pete Candoli (trumpet), Chuck Findley (high trumpet)

MUSIC, MAESTRO, PLEASE!
LEADER: Billy May TRUMPETS: Shorty Sherock, John Best, Uan Rasey TROMBONES: Dick Nash, Lew McCreary SAXOPHONES: Les Robinson, Justin Gordon, Don Raffell,

Chuck Gentry PIANO: Ray Sherman GUITAR: Jack Marshall BASS: Rolly Bundock DRUMS: Nick Fatool SOLOS: Joe Howard (trombone), Abe Most (clarinet), Ray Sherman (celesta), Justin Gordon (tenor saxophone) VOCAL: Eileen Wilson

POWERHOUSE
LEADER: Billy May TRUMPETS: Pete Candoli CLARINET: Abe Most TENOR SAXOPHONE: Justin Gordon PIANO: Ray Sherman BASS: Rolly Bundock DRUMS: Nick Fatool XYLOPHONE: Larry Bunker

I LET A SONG GO OUT OF MY HEART
LEADER: Billy May TRUMPETS: Pete Candoli, Uan Rasey, John Audino TROMBONES: Joe Howard, Lew McCreary, Lloyd Ulyate SAXOPHONES: Skeets Herfurt, Willie Schwartz, Justin Gordon, Jack Nimitz PIANO: Ray Sherman GUITAR: Jack Marshall BASS: Rolly Bundock DRUMS: Nick Fatool SOLOS: Skeets Herfurt (alto saxophone), Jack Nimitz (baritone saxophone), Abe Most (clarinet), Joe Howard (trombone)

CHANGES
LEADER: Billy May TRUMPETS: Pete Candoli, John Best, Uan Rasey TROMBONES: Joe Howard, Dick Nash SAXOPHONES: Les Robinson, Willie Schwartz, Justin Gordon, Don Raffell PIANO: Ray Sherman GUITAR: Jack Marshall BASS: Rolly Bundock DRUMS: Nick Fatool SOLOS: Abe Most (clarinet), Shorty Sherock (trumpet)

BOOGIE WOOGIE
LEADER: Glen Gray TRUMPETS: Shorty Sherock, Manny Klein, Conrad Gozzo, Pete Candoli TROMBONES: Joe Howard, Murray McEachern, Si Zentner, Milt Bernhart SAXOPHONES: Skeets Herfurt, Gus Bivona, Babe Russin, Julie Jacob, Chuck Gentry PIANO: Ray Sherman GUITAR: Jack Marshall BASS: Mike Rubin DRUMS: Nick Fatool SOLOS: Ray Sherman (piano), Joe Howard (trombone)

TWILIGHT IN TURKEY
LEADER: Billy May TRUMPET: Pete Candoli CLARINET: Abe Most TENOR SAXOPHONE: Justin Gordon PIANO: Ray Sherman BASS: Rolly Bundock DRUMS: Nick Fatool FINGER CYMBALS: Larry Bunker

MARGIE
LEADER: Billy May TRUMPETS: Pete Candoli, Shorty Sherock, Uan Rasey TROMBONES: Dick Nash, Lew McCreary SAXOPHONES: Les Robinson, Justin Gordon, Abe Most, Don Lodice, Chuck Gentry PIANO: Ray Sherman GUITAR: Jack Marshall BASS: Rolly Bundock DRUMS: Nick Fatool SOLOS: Les Robinson (alto saxophone), Jack Marshall (guitar), Trummy Young (trombone) VOCAL: Trummy Young

ROLL 'EM
LEADER: Billy May TRUMPETS: Pete Candoli, John Audino, Uan Rasey TROMBONES: Joe Howard, Lew McCreary, Lloyd Ulyate SAXOPHONES: Skeets Herfurt, Plas Johnson, Justin Gordon, Willie Schwartz PIANO: Ray Sherman GUITAR: Jack Marshall BASS: Rolly Bundock DRUMS: Nick Fatool SOLOS: Abe Most (clarinet), Shorty Sherock (trumpet), Ray Sherman (piano)

SOUTH RAMPART STREET PARADE
LEADER: Glen Gray TRUMPETS: Conrad Gozzo, Shorty Sherock, Manny Klein, Pete Candoli TROMBONES: Si Zentner, Murray McEachern, Joe Howard, Benny Benson SAXOPHONES: Skeets Herfurt, Gus Bivona, Babe Russin, Chuck Gentry, Julie Jacob PIANO: Ray Sherman GUITAR: Jack Marshall BASS: Mike Rubin DRUMS: Nick Fatool SOLOS: Gus Bivona (clarinet), Shorty Sherock (trumpet)

ORCHESTRA MANAGER: Abe Siegel
MIXER: Rex Updegraft

Discography

The original recordings of the
selections re-created in this volume

DON'T BE THAT WAY
Composers: Benny Goodman and Edgar Sampson. Arranger: Edgar Sampson. Recorded for Victor February 16, 1938
TRUMPETS: Chris Griffin, Harry James, Ziggy Elman TROMBONES: Vernon Brown, Red Ballard CLARINET: Benny Goodman SAXOPHONES: Hymie Shertzer, George Koenig, Arthur Rollini, °Babe Russin · PIANO: Jess Stacy GUITAR: Allan Reuss BASS: Harry Goodman DRUMS: Gene Krupa

SLEEPY TIME GAL
Composers: Ange Lorenzo and Richard A. Whiting. Arranger: H. Eugene Gifford. Recorded for Decca December 8, 1937
TRUMPETS: Frank Zullo, Grady Watts, Sonny Dunham TROMBONES: Billy Rauch, °Murray McEachern, Pee Wee Hunt SAXOPHONES: Glen Gray, Clarence Hutchenrider, Kenny Sargent, Art Ralston, Danny d'Andrea, Pat Davis PIANO: Joe Hall GUITAR: Jack Burdette BASS: Stanley Dennis DRUMS: Tony Briglia

ANNIE LAURIE
Composer: Lady John Scott. Arranger: Sy Oliver. Recorded for Decca November 5, 1937
TRUMPETS: Eddie Tompkins, Paul Webster, Sy Oliver TROMBONES: Elmer Crumbley, Russell Bowles, °Trummy Young SAXOPHONES: °Willie Smith, Earl Carruthers, Ted Buckner, °Joe Thomas, °Dan Grissom PIANO: Eddie Wilcox GUITAR: Al Norris BASS: Moses Allen DRUMS: Jimmie Crawford

SUMMERTIME
Composer: George Gershwin. Arranger: Deane Kincaide. Recorded for Decca October 21, 1938
TRUMPETS: Zeke Zarchy, Sterling Bose, Billy Butterfield TROMBONES: Ward Silloway, Warren Smith SAXOPHONES: Irving Fazola, Matty Matlock, Gil Rodin, Joe Kearns, Eddie Miller PIANO: Bob Zurke GUITAR: Nappy Lamare BASS: Bob Haggart DRUMS: Ray Bauduc

EVERY TUB
Composers: Count Basie and Eddie Durham. "Head" arrangement. Recorded for Decca February 16, 1938
TRUMPETS: Ed Lewis, Harry Edison, Buck Clayton TROMBONES: Dan Minor, Eddie Durham, Benny Morton SAXOPHONES: Jack Washington, Earle Warren, Herschel Evans, Lester Young PIANO: Count Basie GUITAR: Freddie Green BASS: Walter Page DRUMS: Jo Jones

---

°Took part in one or more of the
re-creations in this volume

BLUE AND SENTIMENTAL
Composer: Count Basie. "Head" arrangement. Recorded for Decca June 6, 1938
Same as EVERY TUB

WHAT IS THIS THING CALLED LOVE?
Composer: Cole Porter. Arranger: Jerry Gray. Recorded for Bluebird July 24, 1938
TRUMPETS: Chuck Peterson, °John Best, Claude Bowen TROMBONES: George Arus, Russ Brown, Harry Rodgers CLARINET: Artie Shaw SAXOPHONES: George Koenig, Hank Freeman, Tony Pastor, Ronny Perry PIANO: Les Burness GUITAR: Al Avola BASS: Sid Weiss DRUMS: Cliff Leeman

THE DIPSY DOODLE
Composer, arranger and lyricist: Larry Clinton. Recorded for Victor October 14, 1937
TRUMPETS: Peewee Erwin, Lee Castaldo, Andy Ferretti TROMBONES: Tommy Dorsey, Les Jenkins, Earle Hagen SAXOPHONES: Johnny Mince, Fred Stulce, °Skeets Herfurt, Anthony Antonelli PIANO: Howard Smith GUITAR: Carmen Mastren BASS: Gene Traxler DRUMS: Dave Tough VOCAL: Edythe Wright

SING, SING, SING: Parts I and II
Composer: Louis Prima. Arranger: Jimmy Mundy. Recorded for Victor July 6, 1937
TRUMPETS: Chris Griffin, Harry James, Ziggy Elman TROMBONES: °Murray McEachern, Red Ballard CLARINET: Benny Goodman SAXOPHONES: Hymie Shertzer, George Koenig, Arthur Rollini, Vido Musso PIANO: Jess Stacy GUITAR: Allan Reuss BASS: Harry Goodman DRUMS: Gene Krupa

---

JOHN'S IDEA
Composers: Count Basie and Eddie Durham. Arranger: Eddie Durham. Recorded for Decca July 7, 1937
TRUMPETS: Ed Lewis, Bobby Moore, Buck Clayton TROMBONES: George Hunt, Dan Minor SAXOPHONES: Jack Washington, Earle Warren, Herschel Evans, Lester Young PIANO: Count Basie GUITAR: Freddie Green BASS: Walter Page DRUMS: Jo Jones

COQUETTE
Composers: Carmen Lombardo and Johnny Green. Arranger: Sy Oliver. Lyricist: Gus Kahn. Recorded for Decca June 15, 1937
TRUMPETS: Eddie Tompkins, Paul Webster, Sy Oliver TROMBONES: Elmer Crumbley, Russell Bowles, Eddie Durham SAXOPHONES: °Willie Smith, Earl Carruthers, Ed Brown, °Joe Thomas, °Dan Grissom PIANO: Eddie Wilcox GUITAR: Al Norris BASS: Moses Allen DRUMS: Jimmie Crawford VOCAL: °Dan Grissom

LIZA
Composer: George Gershwin. Arranger: Benny Carter. Recorded for Decca May 2, 1938
TRUMPETS: Mario Bauza, Bobby Stark, Taft Jordan TROMBONES: Nat Story, Sandy Williams, George Matthews SAXOPHONES: Garvin Bushell, Hilton Jefferson, Teddy McRae, Wayman Carver PIANO: Tommy Fulford GUITAR: Bobby Johnson BASS: Beverly Peer DRUMS: Chick Webb

NIGHTMARE
Composer and arranger: Artie Shaw. Recorded for Brunswick September 17, 1937
TRUMPETS: °John Best, Malcolm Crain, Tom Di Carlo TROMBONES: Harry Rodgers, George Arus CLARINET: Artie Shaw SAXOPHONES: °Les Robinson, Hank Freeman, Tony Pastor, Jules Rubin PIANO: Les Burness GUITAR: Al Avola BASS: Ben Ginsberg DRUMS: Cliff Leeman

MARCH OF THE BOB CATS
Composers: Ray Bauduc, Bob Crosby, Gil Rodin, Bob Haggart, Irving Fazola, Nappy Lamare, Matty Matlock, Eddie Miller. "Head" arrangement. Recorded for Decca March 14, 1938
TRUMPET: Yank Lawson TROMBONE: Warren Smith CLARINET: Irving Fazola TENOR SAXOPHONE: Eddie Miller PIANO: Bob Zurke GUITAR: Nappy Lamare BASS: Haig Stephens DRUMS: Ray Bauduc

---

BACK BAY SHUFFLE
Composers: Teddy McRae and Artie Shaw. Arranger: Teddy McRae. Recorded for Bluebird July 24, 1938
Same as WHAT IS THIS THING CALLED LOVE? except Ted Vesely (trumpet) and °Les Robinson (saxophone) replace Russ Brown and George Koenig.

SMOKE RINGS
Composer and arranger: H. Eugene Gifford. Recorded for Decca July 23, 1937
Same as SLEEPY TIME GAL except Walter Smith (trumpet) and Fritz Hummel (trombone) replace Sonny Dunham and Murray McEachern.

LITTLE ROCK GETAWAY
Composer: Joe Sullivan. Arranger: Matty Matlock. Recorded for Decca November 9, 1937
TRUMPETS: Andy Ferretti, Yank Lawson, Billy Butterfield TROMBONES: Ward Silloway, Warren Smith SAXOPHONES: Matty Matlock, Bill De Pew, Gil Rodin, Joe Kearns, Eddie Miller PIANO: Bob Zurke GUITAR: Nappy Lamare BASS: Bob Haggart DRUMS: Ray Bauduc

I CAN'T GET STARTED
Composer: Vernon Duke. Lyricist: Ira Gershwin. Arranger: Joe Lipman. Recorded for Victor August 7, 1937
TRUMPETS: Bunny Berigan, Irving Goodman, Steve Lipkins TROMBONES: Morey Samel, Sonny Lee SAXOPHONES: Joe Dixon, Mike Doty, Clyde Rounds, George Auld PIANO: Joe Lipman GUITAR: Tom Morgan BASS: Hank Wayland DRUMS: George Wettling VOCAL: Bunny Berigan

QUAKER CITY JAZZ
Composers: Jan Savitt and Jimmy Schultz. Arranger: Jimmy Schultz. Recorded for Bluebird October 21, 1938
TRUMPETS: Jack Hansen, Harold Kearns, Charles Jensen TROMBONES: Maurice Evans, Al Leopold SAXOPHONES: Johnny Warrington, Jimmy Schultz, Gabe Galinas, Harry Roberts PIANO: Irv Leshner BASS: Howard Cook DRUMS: George White

---

FOR DANCERS ONLY
Composer and arranger: Sy Oliver. Recorded for Decca June 15, 1937
Same as COQUETTE without vocalist

MUSIC, MAESTRO, PLEASE!
Composer: Allie Wrubel. Lyricist: Herbert Magidson. Arranger: Axel Stordahl. Recorded for Victor April 27, 1938
TRUMPETS: Peewee Erwin, Lee Castaldo, Andy Ferretti TROMBONES: Tommy Dorsey, Les Jenkins, Earle Hagen SAXOPHONES: Hymie Shertzer, Johnny Mince, °Skeets Herfurt, Deane Kincaide, Fred Stulce PIANO: Howard Smith GUITAR: Carmen Mastren BASS: Gene Traxler DRUMS: Maurice Purtill VOCAL: Edythe Wright

POWERHOUSE
Composer and arranger: Raymond Scott. Recorded for Master February 20, 1937
PIANO: Raymond Scott BASS: Lou Shoobe TRUMPET: Dave Wade CLARINET: Pete Pumiglio: TENOR SAXOPHONE: Dave Harris DRUMS: Johnny Williams, Sr.

I LET A SONG GO OUT OF MY HEART
Composer and arranger: Duke Ellington. Recorded for Brunswick March 3, 1938
TRUMPETS: Wallace Jones, Cootie Williams, Rex Stewart, Harold Baker TROMBONES: Joe Nanton, Juan Tizol, Lawrence Brown SAXOPHONES: Barney Bigard, Otto Hardwick, Johnny Hodges, Harry Carney PIANO: Duke Ellington GUITAR: Fred Guy BASS: Hayes Alvis, Billy Taylor DRUMS: Sonny Greer

CHANGES
Composer: Walter Donaldson. Arranger: Fletcher Henderson. Recorded for Victor July 7, 1937
Same as SING, SING, SING

BOOGIE WOOGIE
Composer: Clarence ("Pinetop") Smith. Arranger: Deane Kincaide. Recorded for Victor September 16, 1938
TRUMPETS: Charlie Spivak, Yank Lawson, Lee Castaldo TROMBONES: Tommy Dorsey, Les Jenkins, Moe Zudekoff SAXOPHONES: Hymie Shertzer, Johnny Mince, Fred Stulce, °Skeets Herfurt, Deane Kincaide PIANO: Howard Smith GUITAR: Carmen Mastren BASS: Gene Traxler DRUMS: Maurice Purtill

TWILIGHT IN TURKEY
Composer and arranger: Raymond Scott. Recorded for Master February 20, 1937
Same as POWERHOUSE

MARGIE
Composers: Con Conrad and J. Russel Robinson. Arranger: Sy Oliver. Lyricist: Benny Davis. Recorded for Decca January 6, 1938
Same as ANNIE LAURIE with vocal by Trummy Young

ROLL 'EM
Composer and arranger: Mary Lou Williams. Recorded for Victor July 7, 1937
Same as SING, SING, SING

SOUTH RAMPART STREET PARADE
Composers: Ray Bauduc and Bob Haggart. Arranger: Bob Haggart. Recorded for Decca November 16, 1937
TRUMPETS: Charlie Spivak, Yank Lawson, Billy Butterfield TROMBONES: Ward Silloway, Warren Smith CLARINET: Matty Matlock, SAXOPHONES: Bill De Pew, Joe Kearns, Eddie Miller PIANO: Bob Zurke GUITAR: Nappy Lamare BASS: Bob Haggart DRUMS: Ray Bauduc

---

ACKNOWLEDGMENTS

For assistance on "Vintage Years of Humor" the editors of TIME-LIFE RECORDS wish to thank the National Cartoonist Society and the Magazine Cartoonist Guild. For picture assistance on other sections of the book, Mira Schachne; for research, Shirley Small; and for captions, Charles Elliot.

Time Inc. departments and staff members who were helpful: Anne Drayton and Carmela Lotrecchiano of the offices of LIFE's Director of Photography; Marcia Gauger and Barbara Wilkins of the Time-Life News Service; Doris O'Neil, Chief of the Time Inc. Picture Collection; George Karas and Herbert Orth of the Photographic Laboratory.

For information on the music, the musicians and related subjects of the period, the editors are particularly indebted to: Ray Bauduc, Al Brackman, Emmett Berry, Harry Carney, Larry Clinton, Helen Dance, Frank Driggs, Sonny Dunham, Eddie Durham, Herb Ellis, Gene Clifford, Douglass Gray, Jerry Gray, Johnny Green, Johnny Guarnieri, Bob Haggart, Dave Harris, Horace Henderson, E. L. Herbst, Joseph Hostetter, Walter ("Pee Wee") Hunt, Clarence Hutchenrider, Dave Kapp, Deane Kincaide, Gene Krupa, Teddy Lee, Joe Lipman, Jack Lomas, Matty Matlock, Teddy McRae, Eddie Miller, Jimmy Mundy, Francis O'Keefe, Sy Oliver, Charles Peterson, Louis Prima, Art Ralston, Frederic Ramsey Jr., Harry Rodgers, Gil Rodin, Arthur Rollini, Edgar Sampson, Ron Sclater, Raymond Scott, Charlie Shavers, Louis Shoobe, Robert Stephens, Gary Stevens, Warren Doyle Smith, Joe Sullivan, Joe Thomas, Dave Wade, Larry Wagner, Earle Warren, Grady Watts, Johnny Williams, Trummy Young.